# Jesus' Dilemma

## Jews are Greeks; Babylon is Rome; Paul is Peter.

(A sequel to the book: British Invented Jesus to Cheat and Win)

## *May all the words here be the word of God*
Angel Gabriel

# <u>Contents</u>



+++

# PREFACE

**A simple man believes anything; a prudent man gives thought to his steps.**
(Proverbs: 14:15)

**Test all things; hold fast what is good.**
(1 Thessalonians: 5:21)

**Beloved, Do not believe every spirit, but test the spirits, whether they are of God, because many false prophets have gone out into the world**
(1 John: 4:1)

**God is not man, that he should lie:  nor a son of man that he should repent, Has He said, and will He not do?  Or has He spoken; will he not make it good?**
(Numbers: 23:19)

Based on the above concepts, the book BRITISH INVENTED JESUS TO CHEAT AND WIN established that a British mastermind with a team of Greeks under him originally wrote all twenty-seven (27) books of the New Testament of the Bible after 1492 AD in the Greek language. They faked their story as though the New Testament was written by a few unschooled Jewish fishermen on scrolls in the first century AD in the Greek language, a language they did not know at all, to be read by Jews.

In short, unschooled Jews wrote it in Greek to be read by Jews. In other words, illiterate Englishmen wrote books for English people to read, not in English but in French.

And they left many footprints of the scam in the process.

The British, along with the West, were selling Bibles and preaching the message of Jesus concurrently as they were engaging in Triple-Sin.

They were faking themselves as good men while doing the worst ever evil.

**We can easily conclude that the story of Jesus in the New Testament is a scam (original scam).**

What about this book?

**This book establishes another scam.**

Another scam was formulated by the scammers to validate the original scam. The enormous funds derived by TripleSinning and collected at the Vatican were used to build monuments concurrently (during the White Golden Era from 1500 to 1900 AD) across the globe to seal and stamp the original scam as accurate. They faked that the monuments built in this era after the fifteenth century were initially built in the fourth century.

So, the original scam falsely claimed that the disciples of Jesus wrote the message of Jesus called the Gospels in the first century AD while they were alive, concealing that truth that a British master mind wrote those after 1492 AD.

Then, the subsequent scam claimed that the monuments built after 1492 D were built initially in the fourth century, concealing that truth that they built those only after 1492 AD.

As we can see from the above evil scheme, no one can prove or disprove these two scams — **or so they thought.**

But as always, in such elaborate scams, they left the footprints of their robbery all along the way.

**In this book, we explore and study their footprints.**

## <u>Jesus and Eternal Life</u>

The offer of Jesus was a place in heaven after your worldly life, which was also not verifiable in life.

Jesus wants you to believe in him blindly, and he offers a prize: only suffering in this life but a special place in heaven.

**Lk. 14:27    And anyone who does not carry his cross and follow me
cannot be my disciple.**

**Lk. 14:33**     In the same way, any of you who does not give up everything he has cannot be my disciple.

**Jn. 11:25**     Jesus said to her, "I am the resurrection and the life. He who believes in me will live, even though he dies;

**Jn. 11:26**     and whoever lives and believes in me will never die. Do you believe this?"

**Jn. 20:29**     Then Jesus told him, "Because you have seen me, you have believed; blessed are those who have not seen and yet have believed."

**The Bible clearly says not to believe anything illogical without verifying the facts, but Jesus wants you to believe him and in him blindly.**

# THE SCAM OF JESUS IS CRYSTAL CLEAR

+++

# HIGHLIGHTS

### GOD OF ABRAHAM IN THREE DRESSES
First, Jews invented the God of Abraham, who loved only Jews and hated all the rest, called the Gentiles.
**This God was angry.**

Then, the British, in Greek dress, invented Jesus, whose father was the God of Abraham, the God of Jews. God of Abraham was dressed differently and had a very distinct character. This God hated Jews for not believing in Jesus and loved all the Gentiles who believed in Jesus.
**This God was loving and forgiving.**

Then, a prophet arose who spoke to the same God of Abraham, and the God agreed to change his dress and his character. This God hated Jews and Christians but loved those who believed in the prophet.
**This God was furious and beheaded all who belittled the prophet.**

### THOU SHALL NOT KILL AND COVET: ALL THEY DO IS KILL AND COVET
All three believers, Jews, Christians, and Muslims, believe in the Ten Commandments, which were given to Moses by the God of Abraham.

All three preached the essence of the Commandments; "Thou shall not kill and covet," but all they did daily was to kill and covet.

### THE WAR GOD, GOD OF ABRAHAM & THE RIGHT TO DEFEND FREEDOM
Since the advent of Jesus, enlisting Christians, all wars have been launched by Christians lately called NATO, a de facto war machine to establish a Christian Caliphate.

All three quietly preached about creating the Caliphate and believed their God would ultimately rule the whole world, the Caliphate.

## <u>THE ULTIMATE CHRISTIAN AGENDA</u>
Christian agenda is to fulfill the message of Jesus:

MAKE THE ENTIRE WORLD A CHRISTIAN CALIPHATE SINCE ALL OTHER GODS ARE FAKE GODS.


## <u>DID THE WEST FORGE WESTERN HISTORY TO SUIT THE AGENDA</u>
Did the British collude with the rest of the West to establish the ultimate building of the Christian Caliphate?

INVADE THE LAND OF OTHERS AND CLAIM THE RIGHT TO DEFEND.

**+++**

Volume 1

# PRAYING TO JESUS TO BLESS THE TRIPLE-SINNING

## Volume 1-Praying to Jesus to Bless the TripleSinning

## Volume 1: Ch 1- The Pope and the Fruit Tree

### HIGHLIGHTS
* Pope's double face: "We hate Muslims, but we love Muslims" *
* Pope lives and works only for cash collection from the believers *
* Every Christian church is the same globally, selling eternal life *
### * Church is all about gaining wealth and prestige *
****************************************

1) The fruit tells you about the tree. (Gospel of Matthew 12: 33).

> *Mt. 12:33*    *"Make a tree good and its fruit will be good, or make a tree bad and its fruit will be bad, for a tree is recognised by its fruit.*

2) What is the fruit of Christianity since Jesus?
3) We can assess it from what the Pope does.
4) What does the Pope do on Good Fridays after years of cash collections, lustful living, and monument building by the clergy attaining the White Golden Era?
5) The Pope washes the feet of three Muslims on that day for the world to see and looks after the Christian party, the party of Jesus.
6) The Pope is displaying a double face: "We hate Muslims & we love Muslims.
7) The Pope makes an exceptional appeal for cash on that day by a worldwide appeal (Ref: a & b).
8) He gives a sermon in the Vatican, reminding the laity about giving to God.
9) That sermon contradicted the teaching of Jesus as he specifically instructed his disciples not to seek cash in serving God.
10) Jesus said in the Gospel of Matthew:

> *Mk. 6:7*    *Calling the Twelve to him, he sent them out two by two and gave them authority over evil [Greek: unclean] spirits.*

> *Mk. 6:8*    *These were his instructions:* **"Take nothing for the journey except a staff — no bread, no bag, no money in your belts.**

> *Mk. 6:9*    *Wear sandals but not an extra tunic.*

11) Eternal life in heaven is on cheap sale now by the Christian church for simple people since "simple people believe anything."
**12) Cash is the aim of the cross; lust is a bonus.**

References:

a) Seeds of the Gospel take time to Bloom: Pope Francis: **https://www.catholicnewsagency.com/news/258019/pope-francis-at-sunday-angelus-the-seeds-of-the-gospel-take-time-to-bloom** Christian Population in Israel: https://www.timesofisrael.com/annual-christmas-report-says-israels-christian-population-has-grown-to-185000/

b) History of Confession is a tale of sexual obsession & exploitation: **https://www.ncronline.org/books/2022/06/history-confession-tale-sexual-obsession-exploitation**

c) Videos, debates, and presentations by Rabbi Michel Skobac in Jews for Judaism; **https://jewsforjudaism.org/staff**

d) Western propaganda on the Bible by highly reputable Jesus-deniers.

e) Those are extensive and argue that the New Testament contains too many anomalies, but there is no fraud or conspiracy in its publication.

f) Those include books, YouTube videos, podcasts, debates etc. on the truth of the story of Jesus:

    i)     By Dr. Bart D. Ehrman: **https://en.wikipedia.org/wiki/Bart_D._Ehrman**

    ii)     By Dr. David Skrbina: **https://www.davidskrbina.com/**

    iii)     By Derek Lambert of MythVision podcasts: **https://www.youtube.com/@MythVisionPodcast**

g) Did Jesus exist: Yes: by Open Mind: **https://www.bbvaopenmind.com/en/science/scientific-insights/did-jesus-of-nazareth-actually-exist-the-evidence-says-yes/**

***

## Volume 1-Praying to Jesus to Bless the TripleSinning

## Volume 1: Ch 2- The White Golden Era

### HIGHLIGHTS
* Christians jointly invented Jesus and concurrently invented TripleSin *
* Christians prayed to Jesus to bless them, and Jusus readily complied *
* The Christian Golden Era arrived *
*** Church is all about gaining wealth and prestige ***
****************************************

1) The most significant money laundering scheme ever is the TripleSin (Slave Trade, colonialism, and Apartheid) run by the Western Christians.
2) But it cannot match their invention of the story of Jesus, which was invented to support and complement the TripleSin.
3) They preached not to kill and not to covet, but they did just that for four centuries: **kill and covet.**
4) **TripleSin was an organized crime organization established and managed by the Pope in the Vatican and the Archbishop of the Church of England, the Anglican Church.**
5) This involvement of the then Archbishop Thomas Secher in the 18th century is now being established by the Lambeth Palace Library, the National Library and Archives of the Church of England, as per one of the latest articles published by the Guardian Newspaper on 25 May 2024 (Ref# c).
6) The article highlighted the following:

   *"The church was at the center of establishing slavery and was probably one of the biggest benefactors."*

7) We must stress the word here; "establishing slavery" rather than participating in Slavery.
8) The Pope was even bolder. According to Wikipedia, the Pope stated the following: (Ref: f).

   *In 1866, the Holy Office of <u>Pope Pius IX</u> stated that, subject to conditions, it was not against <u>divine law</u> for a slave to be sold, bought, or exchanged.*

9) This incredible statement by the then-People came three years after Abraham Lincoln famously or infamously abolished slavery in the USA, meaning that the abolition was an eyewash.
10) They sold a slave for $800 a slave. (Ref# c)
11) An auction of Slaves at Richmond, Virginia, in the USA read: (Ref# c)

> *10 Likely Negroes as ever offered in the market; among them is a man who is a Superior cook and a House Servant, and a girl about seventeen years old, a first-rate House Servant and an excellent seamstress.*

12) The Christian slave trade ran as a legitimate trade for four centuries.
13) The Christian slave trade continued to run for more than a century after the "all men are created equal" speech of President Jefferson.
14) The American constitution declared the concept that all men are created equal, while the slave trade flourished as a proud legacy of America.
15) The Western civilization is founded on the contradiction: "We are holy men of Jesus living on TripleSin."
16) The slave trade alone grossed US$1,000 trillion or more at today's value in four centuries, excluding that derived from Colonialism and Apartheid. (Ref# c-h).
17) That is a conservative figure.
18) The Christians not only stole money, land, trade, and skills of others but also caused the worst human suffering while profiting from the trade. (Ref# c-h).
19) Britain was the poorest country in the world before the TripleSin (Slave Trade, Colonialism, and Apartheid).
20) India was the wealthiest country at those times.
21) And that position reversed when the war was won by the TripleSinners.
22) They won the war with an atomic bomb built from the laundered money in the USA.
23) Britain, the biggest looter, became the richest, with France, Italy, and America close behind.
24) The big-time robbers changed their dress after the war and became world policemen and human rights champions, preaching equal rights.
25) Spreading the word of Jesus and collecting cash for Jesus continued with increased vigor, led first by the British and now by the Americans.
26) Jesus enabled this miracle: cash-rich robbers donning the silk of the Pope, King, and President unilaterally decide "right and wrong," creating the "rule-based world order."
27) After the White Golden Era, from 1600 AD to 2000 AD, the Anglican world, the British world, or the Commonwealth, now known as AUKUS, became the richest, deviously stealing the wealth of the rest in Jesus's name.
28) They proudly and loudly spread the word of Jesus.
29) And Jesus blessed them so much that they became so rich that Jesus would not let them into Heaven.
30) Rich people are not admitted to Heaven.
31) Jesus said in chapter 19 of the Gospel of Matthew:

| | |
|---|---|
| *Mt. 19:23* | *Then Jesus said to his disciples, "I tell you the truth, it is hard for a rich man to enter the kingdom of heaven.* |
| *Mt. 19:24* | *Again I tell you, it is easier for a camel to go through the eye of a needle than for a rich man to enter the kingdom of God."* |
| *Mt. 19:25* | *When the disciples heard this, they were greatly astonished and asked, "Who then can be saved?"* |
| *Mt. 19:26* | *Jesus looked at them and said, "With man this is impossible, but with God all things are possible."* |
| *Mt. 19:27* | *Peter answered him, "We have left everything to follow you! What then will there be for us?"* |
| *Mt. 19:28* | *Jesus said to them, "I tell you the truth, at the renewal of all things, when the Son of Man sits on his glorious throne, you who have followed me will also sit on twelve thrones, judging the twelve tribes of Israel.* |
| *Mt. 19:29* | *And everyone who has left houses or brothers or sisters or father or mother [Some manuscripts: mother or wife] or children or fields for my sake will receive a hundred times as much and will inherit eternal life.* |
| *Mt. 19:30* | *But many who are first will be last, and many who are last will be first.* |

32) What did the White Anglican AUKUS achieve in this Golden Era? (volumes 3, 4 & 5)
33) They invented Jesus and the Trinity, three gods in one god.
34) Simultaneously, they launched TripleSin.
35) Simultaneously, they sent missionaries to sell the Bible as messengers of Jesus. (Ref# c-h).
36) They made a rule that laity should confess every Sunday and give God 10% of their income for the forgiveness of the sins committed the previous week (**chaining and selling slaves, including *seventeen-year-old girls***)
37) People contributed billions of US dollars to the kitty of the Vatican and Canterbury.
**38)** The Pope and Archbishop spent 10% on good things, stole 50% for family expenses, and invested 40% in building monuments to collect tourist money into the same kitty.
**39)** They also prayed jointly to Jesus to bless their project, **Jesus Christ.**
40) The monuments are on display worldwide, reminding us of the grace of Jesus. (Ref# a-h)
41) Those monuments still gross significant daily income.
42) As a bonus, celibate bishops and cardinals used virgins and boys for extracurricular activities. (Ref# c-h).
43) Old stories of lust are coming out daily and weekly, but the Pope is trying to hide them.
44) They invested in the atom bomb, won the war, and appointed them as trustees of the United Nations.
45) And the world glorified the liberty, freedom, and human rights brought to you by the TripleSinners by the grace of Jesus, standing tall for the worst sinners.
46) Jesus proclaimed in the Gospels: chapter 20 of the Gospel of John (typical of the four Gospels)

*Jn. 20:29*     *Then Jesus told him, "Because you have seen me, you have believed; blessed are those who have not seen and yet have believed."*

47) Jesus truly rewarded the believers as promised: "**Believe in me and be blessed.**"

References:

a) See the illustrations attached in this chapter.
b) Monument building with Proceeds of Crime by the church: See Volumes 3, 4 and 5
c) The TransAtlantic Slave Trade: Equal Justice Initiative: **https://eji.org/report/transatlantic-slave-trade/virginia/#the-domestic-slave-trade**
d) Revealed: How Church of England's ties to chattel slavery to top of hierarchy: **https://www.theguardian.com/world/article/2024/may/25/revealed-how-church-of-englands-ties-to-chattel-slavery-went-to-top-of-hierarchy**
e) The American Contradiction: https://www.socialstudies.org/system/files/2020-06/se_8402076.pdf
f) Slavery, the American Revolution, and the Constitution: https://www.digitalhistory.uh.edu/active_learning/explorations/revolution/revolution_slavery.cfm
g) De-romanticizing American Slavery: https://eji.org/news/history-racial-injustice-deromanticizing-american-slavery/
h) Catholic Church and slavery: Wikipedia: **https://en.wikipedia.org/wiki/Catholic_Church_and_slavery**

***

# The White Golden Era- Slave Trade

<u>The Statue of Liberty</u>
proudly built on

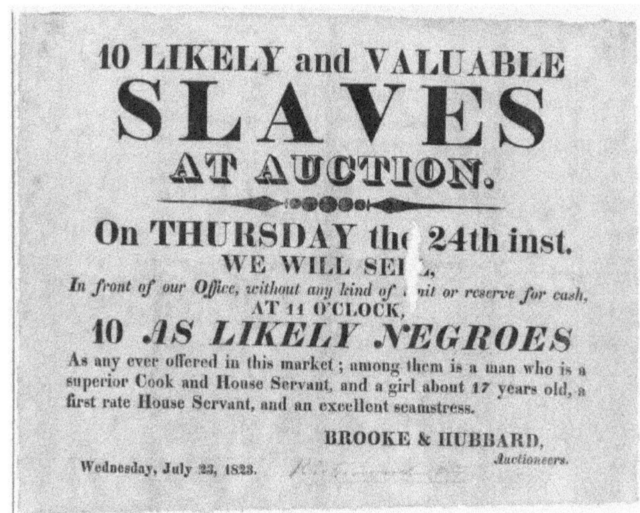

Slave Trade
(See  **https://eji.org/report/transatlantic-slave-trade/** )

# <u>The White Golden Era- Colonialism</u>

<u>Mount Mary Basilica, Bandra, Mumbai, India</u>
proudly built on

<u>Colonialism</u>
(See  **https://en.wikipedia.org/wiki/Colonial_India** &
**https://en.wikipedia.org/wiki/Colonialism** )

# The White Golden Era- Apartheid

**Voortrekker Monument, Pretoria, South Africa**
Proudly built on Apartheid.

(See **https://en.wikipedia.org/wiki/Apartheid** )

**Jesus' Dilemma: Jews are Greeks, Babylon is Rome, Paul is Peter**

Volume 2

# DEFENDING THE UNDEFENDABLE BY THE CHRISTIANS

## Volume 2-Defending the Undefendable by Christians

## Volume 2: Ch 1- The Fake Conduct of Christians.

### HIGHLIGHTS
* There are far too many slips, lies, spins, and tricks in the New Testament *
* Why should anybody spin a story to invent a god? *
* We can see that looting, exploiting, and killing have become the routine conduct of the Christians after inventing Jesus *
* Did the West invent the story of Jesus to portray themselves as good people while looting? *
***A Study and Research on the Story of Jesus and the church is a necessity ***
**************************************

1. Before we discuss the subsequent conduct of Christians for the last many centuries after falsifying the New Testament after 1492 AD, we should briefly summarize the scam in the New Testament established in the book **"British Invented Jesus to Cheat and Win."**

2. That book establishes the crucial point with countless pointers and proof that a mastermind working under the British monarchy wrote all the original twenty-seven books of the New Testament after 1492.

3. The Mastermind acted as seven Jews, as disciples of Jesus, writing testimony in the first century AD.

4. Strangely, those Jewish actors did not write those in the Jewish language but in the Greek language.

5. All those were written not in their language or the language of the intended readers.

6. We are groomed to believe that those unschooled fishermen wrote all those in their own hands-on scrolls, not on modern paper, in a language they had never even heard of.

7. The new story in the New Testament, demoting Mother Mary and promoting her son Jesus as the Son of God, enabled the final formation of the Anglican church in Canterbury, UK.

8. The game was classical British.

9. It was a game of exploiting weaker humans or inferior people, as they called it.

10. It was the turn of the losing Italians to be exploited.

11. It enabled diverting a sizable portion of the vast and ever-increasing loot collected at the Vatican to Canterbury in the UK in 1548.

12. The Vatican loot was easy cash, mainly contributed by and derived from the American Slave trade, one arm of The TripleSin, mainly as taxes to God.

13. The claim or the proposition that the British invented Jesus is rooted in circumstantial, coincidental, motivational evidence reinforced by the immediate actions of the British.
14. Evidence proves that the Anglican church sent English Anglican bishops to all their colonies soon after 1650 AD. (Ref: a & b).
15. They spread the message of Jesus by printing Bibles in local languages and establishing Anglican churches in the colonies, supplementing the erstwhile loot in Europe.
16. The Christian bishops were assigned to mix Jesus with the TripleSin, preaching Jesus on one side when their brothers in military uniforms were killing people to pocket their cash on the other side.
17. That was their immediate action after inventing Jesus, spreading the Anglican version of the story of Jesus.
18. As to the motivation, the British were motivated, but Jews and Greeks had no incentive to invent such a story.
19. Clearly, the sizable easy loot got diverted from the Vatican in Rome to Canterbury in Britain.
20. Looting had become the trade of Britain by 1500 AD.
21. The evidence provided by the West adds to the idea of British arrogance and superiority. (Ref: f, g & h).
22. The motivation was also to establish the British's growing superiority in the TripleSin over the Italians.
23. British kings were not prepared to report and submit to the Italian Pope: Slave masters submitting to slaves. (Ref: f, g & h).
24. The actual timing of the writing of the New Testament after 1492 coincided with the formation of the Anglican church, which started in 1442 and formalized in 1555. (Ref: a, b & c).
25. Circumstances of the Triple Sin, mixing Jesus with the worst exploitation of the British, supports the idea of faking to portray robbers as agents of God.
26. All these tricks have a common trait: misleading the world with propaganda.
27. The British misled the world that the only reason for the creation of the Anglican church, stretching over a century, was to enable King Henry VI to divorce his wife and marry his new lover. (Ref: f, g, h).
28. Similarly, the British very successfully misled people into thinking that the New Testament and the story of Jesus were written by the then-living Apostles in the first century AD, negating the evidence of coincidence.
29. Roman and Jewish history were manipulated to validate the story of Jesus, with millions of stories appearing over the last millennium and still ongoing.
30. They invented Herod the Great and his dynasty to validate the story of Jesus and fell into the ditch.
31. The character of Herod the Great was created to substantiate that Jesus was born while Herod the Great was ruling Judea.
32. As the story evolved, they fell into the ditch. Herod the Great died four years before Jesus was born.
33. Such blunders occur when history is manufactured in the British mill.

34. As Apostle John stated in the last verse of his Gospel, the world will not have enough room to contain all these fake stories invented by Christians to justify their scams.
35. Ivy League scholars are self-declared as the only seekers of the universal truth.
36. They invent stories daily, discover new evidence, and conduct new research validating the Bible and Biblical gods.
37. And they are daily inventing stories to destroy all other gods.
38. Having laid the foundation of the scam as detailed above, we deal with the actual evidence of the fraud, established in the book **"British Invented Jesus to Cheat and Win."**
39. For easy reference, four documents in the book are included, in this book, as follows.
    a. Volume 6 - The Ultimate Truth.
    b. Volume 7- Lies, Spins and Tricks.
    c. Volume 8- Selling Eternal Life for cash.
    d. Volume 9- Maps and Illustrations
40. The New Testament story has a plot to portray that Apostle Paul, not Apostle Peter, established the Roman Orthodox church in Rome in the first century AD, presumably the oldest Christian church.
41. That story defied Jesus, who had appointed Apostle Peter as the **"rock of the church."**
42. A Christian story now contradicts the New Testament, stating that Apostle Peter established the church in Rome and was the first Pope (Ref: i & j).
43. That is a fake attempt to justify the New Testament in a contradictory way, that Apostle Paul did not establish it, but Apostle Peter did.
44. This Christian plot is presented in more detail in chapter 7 of volume 2 of this book, **Paul is Peter.**
45. In the plot of the New Testament, Apostle Paul weaves a story that he, as Apostle of the Gentiles, would establish the church in Rome.
46. Remember that the Roman Catholic church flourished after the fourteenth century when the British mastermind wrote the fake story.
47. Therefore, the British plot or the Anglican plot was to tie the creation of the Roman Orthodox church in the first century AD to Jesus and his Apostles, thereby validating the story of Jesus.
48. Apostle Paul made a terrible but unwanted blunder in weaving that plot.
49. In the Epistle to Romans, Apostle Paul mentioned the word or name "Spain" two times without any real context.
50. But the term or name or country "Spain" did not exist until 1492 AD, exposing that the story was written after 1492 AD.
51. Christians and Ivy League scholars may devise a story to validate the slip, the big blunder.
52. Apostle John, the infamous *Disciple whom Jesus loved* made another serious blunder with devastating effect.
53. Apostle John mentions the word paper once in his "Epistle to Nobody" in 2 John verse 12.
54. That is a colossal slip since the paper was invented in China only in the second century AD.

55. The paper or the word paper was not known in the Middle East until many years after the Eighth century AD. (Ref: k).
56. British and Americans are talented to destroy that undefendable truth, too.
57. We have more evidence to test the British-run America Has Talent drama.
58. The fact that the mastermind of the New Testament had meddled with and defiled prophesies in the Old Testament is undeniable, as presented in volume 4 of the earlier book.
59. This can be easily tested in any Supreme Court of the AUKUS.
60. Similarly, the mastermind copied sentences and paragraphs from Gospels to Gospels, as presented in volume 5 of the earlier book.
61. This copying process can be easily seen and understood.
62. This is undefendable.
63. This can also be tested in any Supreme Court of AUKUS.
64. This copying conduct proves the masterminding theory: the same person or team wrote all four Gospels and progressively corrected, edited, and polished the earlier version.
65. Finally, let us climb to the mountaintop.
66. This deals with the fact that "**Jews are Greek**".
67. Embalming or applying spices to bodies for burial, delaying the decomposition of the body to earth, is prohibited by Jewish Law.
68. None of the Jewish characters, all professing as experts in Jewish Law as depicted in the New Testament, knew it.
69. This blunder is presented with more details in this book in chapter 5 in volume 2, titled *Jews are Greeks*.
70. **With all these slips, lies, spins, and tricks exposed (see also volume 6), the story of Jesus has become undefendable.**


References:


a) Anglicanism: Wikipedia: **https://en.wikipedia.org/wiki/Anglicanism**
b) A brief History of the Anglican Church: All Saints Anglican Church: **https://www.allsaintsspringfield.org/history-of-the-anglican-church.html**
c) Church of England: History. Com: **https://www.history.com/topics/european-history/church-of-england**
d) Church Mission Society: Wikipedia: **https://en.wikipedia.org/wiki/Church_Mission_Society**
e) Timeline of Christian Mission: Wikipedia: **https://en.wikipedia.org/wiki/Timeline_of_Christian_missions**
f) Arrogance of Empire: Paul Foot: Guardian: **https://www.theguardian.com/politics/2003/aug/20/foreignpolicy.usa**
g) British Ignorance and Arrogance: New York Times: **https://www.nytimes.com/1861/07/16/archives/british-ignorance-and-arrogance.html**
h) Queen's Chinese Gaffe shows that imperial arrogance dies hard: **https://theconversation.com/queens-chinese-gaffe-shows-that-imperial-arrogance-dies-hard-59275**
i) Saint Peter: Wikipedia: **https://en.wikipedia.org/wiki/Saint_Peter**
j) What the Early Church believed: Peter as Pope: **https://www.catholic.com/tract/origins-of-peter-as-pope**

k) History of paper by American Forest & Paper Association: **https://www.afandpa.org/news/2021/history-paper#:~:text=About%202%2C000%20years%20ago%2C%20inventors,Lun%2C%20a%20Chinese%20court%20official**

l) Videos, debates, and presentations by Rabbi Michel Skobac in Jews for Judaism; **https://jewsforjudaism.org/staff**

m) Western propaganda on the Bible by highly reputable Jesus-deniers.

n) Those are extensive and argue that the New Testament contains too many anomalies, but there is no fraud or conspiracy in its publication.

o) Those include books, YouTube videos, podcasts, debates etc. on the truth of the story of Jesus:

    i) By Dr. Bart D. Ehrman: **https://en.wikipedia.org/wiki/Bart_D._Ehrman**

    ii) By Dr. David Skrbina: **https://www.davidskrbina.com/**

    iii) By Derek Lambert of MythVision podcasts: **https://www.youtube.com/@MythVisionPodcast**

p) Did Jesus exist: Yes: by Open Mind: **https://www.bbvaopenmind.com/en/science/scientific-insights/did-jesus-of-nazareth-actually-exist-the-evidence-says-yes/**

***

## <u>Volume 2-Defending the Undefendable by Christians</u>

## <u>Volume 2: Ch 2- The Conduct of the Current Christians.</u>

### <u>HIGHLIGHTS</u>
* Christians are desperate to prove that the story of Jesus is not a scam *
* They are engaging in a collective conduct of spinning lies beyond comprehension *
* They engage in such a false conduct, knowing that it is indeed a scam *
* They know that their well-being is founded on Jesus *
***A Study and Research on the Christian Church is a necessity***
******************************************

1) The story of Jesus in the New Testament is an Epic scam criminally conceived by the British under the direction of the British monarchy.

2) This book deals with Christians' long-standing and ongoing conduct defending the undefendable Jesus.

3) In addition, it also deals with their conduct of crucifying all other gods other than Jesus.

4) Their combined game or conspiracy is to write so many contradictory lies that it becomes too complex to decipher the truth.

5) This book is a sequel to the earlier published book, "**British invented Jesus to cheat and win.**"

6) The book established beyond defense that the story of Jesus, collated in the twenty-seven books of the New Testament of the Bible, is a scam to deceive the world.

7) The British and the West reaped gold using this scam directly and indirectly.

8) They collected easy cash for centuries from the vulnerable laity and built monuments and noble institutions from East to West to seal the scam as accurate.

9) They used those to paint them as noblemen while engaging in the worst exploitation of human history for four long centuries of the **White Golden Era**.

10) Finally, they self-appointed them as policemen of the world by force and persuasion.

11) The bully British changed their name to Americans and became the world bully, with the rest of the Whites, including the British, serving as their runners.

12) The book established not only that the British used Greeks, pretending to be Jews, to write these twenty-seven books inventing a god called Jesus but also that the West

collectively created and falsified Western history, mainly Roman and Jewish history, to validate the scam.

13) They built monumental churches and created songs, epic paintings, movies, novels, and millions of fake stories to make and portray the scam as authentic and genuine.

14) They made "coveting and killing of native Americans" a noble and heroic act by the Western movies of John Wayne and Clint Eastwood.

15) They continue to defend the undefendable and derive benefit from it.

16) The current game is to conceal the truth that the story of Jesus is a scam by telling more lies progressively.

17) And inventing more evidence with more research and excavations to complicate the scam beyond comprehension.

18) This is achieved by the noble and the faithful, mainly the Ivy League scholars from the heartland of Christians, the USA, Canada, Britain, Australia, and New Zealand, now named AUKUS.

19) **This book is to record and expose this Epic scam, a scam created to sustain the scam of Jesus.**

References:

a) Videos, debates and presentations by Rabbi Michel Skobac in Jews for Judaism; **https://jewsforjudaism.org/staff**
b) Western propaganda on the Bible by highly reputable Jesus-deniers.
c) Those are extensive and argue that the New Testament contains too many anomalies, but there is no fraud or conspiracy in its publication.
d) Those include books, YouTube videos, podcasts, debates etc. on the truth of the story of Jesus:
   i) By Dr. Bart D. Ehrman: **https://en.wikipedia.org/wiki/Bart_D._Ehrman**
   ii) By Dr. David Skrbina: **https://www.davidskrbina.com/**
   iii) By Derek Lambert of MythVision podcasts: **https://www.youtube.com/@MythVisionPodcast**

e) Did Jesus exist: Yes: by Open Mind: **https://www.bbvaopenmind.com/en/science/scientific-insights/did-jesus-of-nazareth-actually-exist-the-evidence-says-yes/**

***

## <u>Volume 2-Defending the undefendable by Christians</u>

## <u>Volume 2: Ch 3- Blatant Lie of Jesus</u>

### <u>HIGHLIGHTS</u>
* Jesus lied to make him the Messiah *
* Jesus puts words into the mouth of Moses *
* Christians invent lame excuses daily to sustain the lie of Jesus *
***The Lie of Jesus would remain as lie of God of the West ***
*******************************************

1) One of the many ways the British mastermind groomed the world to believe in Jesus and to portray that Jesus was the Messiah of the Jews was to misuse the prophecies contained in the Old Testament.

2) The mastermind amended the texts to mislead the readers, hoping the laity would not verify the prophecies.

3) That idea was destroyed in volume 4 of the book **British Invented Jesus to Cheat and Win**, which analyzed many misquoted prophecies.

4) Most of those defiled prophecies were quoted by the Gospel writers and not directly by Jesus.

5) They made others state that Jesus was the Messiah, and invariably, Jesus commended them for their certification of him being the Messiah, asking them to keep it secret.

6) There is only one prophesy, which Jesus himself portrayed as quoting.

7) Jesus is said to have said it in self-certifying himself as Messiah.

8) Jesus did not say it while alive, but only after his resurrection.

9) It is essential to highlight that God, appearing to many, did not state that Jesus was the Messiah, but instead, God consistently proclaimed that Jesus was his son.

10) **They are worlds apart, son of God and Messiah.**

11) **Let us leave the blunder of the Jewish God and focus on the words of Jesus.**

12) The words spoken by Jesus expose the fraud.

13) Moreover, Christians inventing stories and assertions to validate the fraud uttered by Jesus prove the ever-running conspiracy of the Christians. (Ref: a, b, c, d, e, f, g, h)

14) In simple terms, Jesus claimed that Moses had said Jesus was the Messiah.

15) Paraphrasing Jesus, Jesus said, "Have you not heard that Moses has said that I am the Messiah."

16) Internet and Christian documentation are complete justification for this scam.

17) This is a scam, and it can be easily understood by those who think logically, as the Bible requires.

18) Jesus appeared to the disciples after his resurrection in chapter 24 of the Gospel of Luke.

19) After his death, Jesus had to explain to his twelve disciples that he was the Messiah because he had failed to say directly to them while alive.

20) Jesus said this in the Gospel of Luke very deviously stating this.

> Lk. 24:44    *He said to them, "This is what I told you while I was still* *with you: Everything must be fulfilled that is written about me in the* *Law of Moses, the Prophets and the Psalms."*

> Lk. 24:45    *Then he opened their minds so they could understand the* *Scriptures.*

> Lk. 24:46    *He told them, "This is what is written: The Christ will suffer* *and rise from the dead on the third day,*

> Lk. 24:47    *and repentance and forgiveness of sins will be preached in his* *name to all nations, beginning at Jerusalem.*

> Lk. 24:48    *You are witnesses of these things.*

> Lk. 24:49    *I am going to send you what my Father has promised; but stay in* *the city until you have been clothed with power from on high."*

21) The first thing to note here is that, unlike other verses, there is no mention where such a prophesy may be found in the Old Testament.

22) **Jesus lied blatantly since no such words or verses exist in the Old Testament.**

23) Current Christians create more lies to solidify the lie stated by Jesus.

24) As per the current Christians, this is what Moses said in the Old Testament:

> De. 18:17    *The LORD said to me: "What they say is good.*

> De. 18:18    *I will raise up for them a prophet like you from among their brothers; I will put my words in* *his mouth, and he will tell them everything I command him.*

> De. 18:19    *If anyone does not listen to my words that the prophet speaks in my name, I myself will call* *him to account.*

> De. 18:20    *But a prophet who presumes to speak in my name anything I have not commanded him to* *say, or a prophet who speaks in the name of other gods, must be put to death."*

> De. 18:21    *You may say to yourselves, "How can we know when a message has not been spoken by the* *LORD?"*

> De. 18:22    *If what a prophet proclaims in the name of the LORD does not take place or come true,* *that is a message the LORD has not spoken. That prophet has spoken presumptuously.* *Do not be afraid of him.*

25) Those who read the Old Testament regularly know that the common theme in the Old Testament is that someone, a prophet, would rise to right the sinning Jews.

26) **A prophet and Messiah are worlds apart.**

27) Nothing in these words corroborates what Jesus blatantly claimed.

28) If anything, Jesus was not presented as a prophet in the New Testament but as the Son of God or God.

29) Christians and Jews believe that many such prophets have since arisen.
30) Jesus accepted the prophets Jeremiah and Isaiah.
31) Jesus's utterance of the above words is devious, as it can be used to mislead the laity.
32) There are more lies propagated by Christians to solidify the blatant lie of Jesus.
33) That is not the only misleading justification cited by Christians to justify the blatant lie of Jesus.
34) Some justification appears and disappears from the internet. (Ref: a, b, c, d, e, f, g, h)
35) There is no end: millions or billions are prepared to crucify themselves to justify anything about Jesus by hook or crook.
36) Why?
37) Sustaining the scam of Jesus invented by the British benefits the West enormously.
38) **Notwithstanding the deceptive game of Christians to mislead the naïve & simple, the lie of Jesus would remain as the lie of the God of the West.**

References:

a) Did Jesus claim to be the Messiah? Israel my Glory: **https://israelmyglory.org/article/q-did-jesus-claim-to-be-the-messiah/**

b) If Jesus never called himself God, How did he become one: **https://www.npr.org/transcripts/300246095#:~:text=And%20so%20when%20Jesus%20told,was%20supposed%20to%20be%20God**

c) Christ Revealed in Moses: The Exalted Christ: **https://www.theexaltedchrist.com/exalting-christ-jesus/testimony-of-moses-about-the-christ**

d) Why Messiah must be God: One for Israel: **https://www.oneforisrael.org/bible-based-teaching-from-israel/why-messiah-must-be-god/ian**

e) Messiah 4: Prophets like Moses: **https://www.livius.org/articles/religion/messiah/messiah-5-prophet-like-moses/#:~:text=Moses%20said%3A%20%22The%20Lord%20your,more%2C%20or%20we%20will%20die**

f) Did Moses really write about Jesus? By Eric Chabot: **https://www.cjfm.org/blog/2018/06/11/did-moses-really-write-about-jesus-look-messianic-prophecy-torah/**

g) What did Moses write about Jesus? Christianity: **https://christianity.stackexchange.com/questions/7118/where-did-moses-write-about-jesus**

h) Did Jesus exist: Yes: by Open Mind: **https://www.bbvaopenmind.com/en/science/scientific-insights/did-jesus-of-nazareth-actually-exist-the-evidence-says-yes/**

***

# <u>Volume 2-Defending the undefendable by Christians</u>

## <u>Volume 2: Ch 4- God's Fake Love</u>

### <u>HIGHLIGHTS</u>
* The God loved only Jews and hated Gentiles as per the Bible *
* According to God, God sent Jesus to the world to rule Jews for eternity *
* God did not send Jesus to save the world or to be crucified *
* But as per Apostle John, God sent Jesus to save the word *
* Because God loved the world so much *
* Yet, God would give eternal life only to those who believe in Jesus *
***New Testament is a collection of lies to steal cash of others ***
******************************************

1) Apostle John stated in chapter 3 of his Gospel the following:

> *Jn. 3:14*     *Just as Moses lifted up the snake in the desert, so the Son of Man must be lifted up,*

> *Jn. 3:15*     *that everyone who believes in him may have eternal life. [Or believes may have eternal life in him]*

> *Jn. 3:16*     **"For God so loved the world that he gave his one and only Son,** *[Or his only begotten Son] that whoever believes in him shall not perish but have eternal life.*

> *Jn. 3:17*     *For God did not send his Son into the world to condemn the world, but to save the world through him.*

> *Jn. 3:18*     *Whoever believes in him is not condemned, but whoever does not believe stands condemned already because he has not believed in the name of God's one and only Son. [Or God's only begotten Son]*

> *Jn. 3:19*     *This is the verdict: Light has come into the world, but men loved darkness instead of light because their deeds were evil.*

2) Apostle John claims that God sent Jesus only because God loved the world so much that those who believed in Jesus would have eternal life.
3) But God said something different.
4) The Gospel of Luke states in the first chapter:

> *Lk. 1:30*     *But the angel said to her, "Do not be afraid, Mary, you have found favour with God.*

> *Lk. 1:31*     *You will be with child and give birth to a son, and you are to give him the name Jesus.*

> *Lk. 1:32*     **He will be great and will be called the Son of the Most High. The Lord God will give him the throne of his father David,**

> *Lk. 1:33*     **and he will reign over the house of Jacob for ever; his kingdom will never end."**

> *Lk. 1:34*    "How will this be," Mary asked the angel, "since I am a virgin?"
>
> *Lk. 1:35*    The angel answered, "The Holy Spirit will come upon you, and the power of the Most High will overshadow you. So the holy one to be born will be called [Or So the child to be born will be called holy,] the Son of God.
>
> *Lk. 1:36*    Even Elizabeth your relative is going to have a child in her old age, and she who was said to be barren is in her sixth month.
>
> *Lk. 1:37*    For nothing is impossible with God."
>
> *Lk. 1:38*    "I am the Lord's servant," Mary answered. "May it be to me as you have said." Then the angel left her.

5) God sent Jesus to reign as a king or ruler of Jews for eternity.
6) God was only concerned with Jews as God hated Gentiles who were not circumcised as per the Bible.
7) Clearly, God sent Jesus only to rule Jews to eternity, not to give eternal life to anyone.
8) Would we believe God or Apostle John?
9) **This lie of Apostle John is just one of the many in the Word of God, the New Testament.**
10) **The Gospel of John is full of lies and trickery to mislead the world to collect cash from the world. (Ref: a, b, c, d, & e)**


References:

a) Revealed: How Church of England's ties to chattel slavery to top of hierarchy: **https://www.theguardian.com/world/article/2024/may/25/revealed-how-church-of-englands-ties-to-chattel-slavery-went-to-top-of-hierarchy**
b) The American Contradiction: https://www.socialstudies.org/system/files/2020-06/se_8402076.pdf
c) Slavery, the American Revolution, and the Constitution: https://www.digitalhistory.uh.edu/active_learning/explorations/revolution/revolution_slavery.cfm
d) De-romanticizing American Slavery: https://eji.org/news/history-racial-injustice-deromanticizing-american-slavery/
e) Catholic Church and slavery: Wikipedia: **https://en.wikipedia.org/wiki/Catholic_Church_and_slavery**
f) Videos, debates, and presentations by Rabbi Michel Skobac in Jews for Judaism; **https://jewsforjudaism.org/staff**
g) Western propaganda on the Bible by highly reputable Jesus-deniers.
h) Those are extensive and argue that the New Testament contains too many anomalies, but there is no fraud or conspiracy in its publication.
i) Those include books, YouTube videos, podcasts, debates etc. on the truth of the story of Jesus:
    i) By Dr. Bart D. Ehrman: **https://en.wikipedia.org/wiki/Bart_D._Ehrman**
    ii) By Dr. David Skrbina: **https://www.davidskrbina.com/**
    iii) By Derek Lambert of MythVision podcasts: **https://www.youtube.com/@MythVisionPodcast**
j) Did Jesus exist: Yes: by Open Mind: **https://www.bbvaopenmind.com/en/science/scientific-insights/did-jesus-of-nazareth-actually-exist-the-evidence-says-yes/**

***

## <u>Volume 2-Defending the undefendable by Christians</u>

### <u>Volume 2: Ch 5- Jews are Greeks.</u>

<u>**HIGHLIGHTS**</u>
* The story of Jesus in the New Testament praises the embalming of bodies for burial *
* Every Jewish character depicted as an expert of Jewish Law endorsed this practice *
* Embalming of bodies for burial is strictly prohibited by Jewish Law *
* On the other hand, Greeks do embalm bodies for burial as a routine *
***Jews are Greeks ***
**************************************

1) The inescapable blunder of the Mastermind of the story of Jesus is the extensive embalming of the body of Jesus for his burial.

2) Even today, Jews practice the following customs in general.

3) Jews strictly prohibit embalming or applying spices to bodies for burials, specifically not to delay the decomposition of the body. (Ref: a-g)

4) On the other hand, Greeks embalm and apply spices on the dead bodies for burial. (Ref: a-g)

5) Jews prohibit visitations to the graves for one year of burial. (Ref: a-g)

6) On the other hand, Greeks practice visiting graves immediately after the burial.

7) Jews prohibit opening the graves or the caskets of dead people.

8) On the other hand, Greeks apply or pour perfumes from alabaster jars to the dead bodies after burial during the visitations. (Ref: a-g)

9) We can easily deduce that none of the characters in the New Testament are Jews but Greeks from the following events described in the New Testament.

10) Jesus endorsed and praised when women poured perfumes on Jesus and massaged Jesus.

11) Jesus announced that the anointing prepared his body for burial in all four Gospels.

**12) Jesus was not a Jew but a Greek actor.**

13) All those present, including the twelve disciples, did not object to Jesus's claim that anointing was according to the Jewish burial custom.

**14) All of those were Greek actors and not Jews.**

15) Joseph of Arimathea and Nicodemus together applied seventy-five pounds of spices to prepare Jesus's body for burial, as the Gospel of John states.

**16) Both were not Jews but Greeks.**

17) Mary Magdalene and other women visited the tomb or the grave of Jesus the third day after the burial and brought spices to apply on the body of Jesus.

**18) They were not Jews but Greeks.**

19) It is important to note that there are many Jews today who have converted to Christianity, particularly in the USA.
20) Many are IVY LEAGUE scholars, but they remain silent on this enormous evidence proving the scam of the story of Jesus.
21) While millions invent stories to validate Jesus, nobody has invented any story on this undefendable proof of the scam.
22) **Instead, all, including Jews, remain silent and hide the truth to sustain the scam.**


References:

a) Embalming (preserving body from decaying by applying spices) of body for burial is prohibited by Jewish Law: Rabbi Michael Pont: **https://images.shulcloud.com/1220/uploads/MJCdeathmourningbooklet.pdf**

b) Burial customs of Jews: Rohatyn Jewish Heritage & **https://rohatynjewishheritage.org/en/culture/death-burial-mourning/**

c) Burial customs of Jews: **www.shiva.com** & **https://www.shiva.com/learning-center/death-and-mourning/jewish-funerals-and-burial**

d) Burial Customs of Greeks: **https://en.m.wikipedia.org/wiki/Ancient_Greek_funeral_and_burial_practices#**

e) Neshama: **https://neshamajfs.com/faq/**

f) Ancient Greek funeral and burial practices: **https://en.m.wikipedia.org/wiki/Ancient_Greek_funeral_and_burial_practices**

g) Researchers uncover Roman Greek Embalming practices: **https://cordis.europa.eu/article/id/29846-researchers-uncover-roman-greek-embalming-practices#:~:text=According%20to%20Swiss%20and%20Greek,the%20Journal%20of%20Archaeological%20Science**

h) Videos, debates, and presentations by Rabbi Michel Skobac in Jews for Judaism; **https://jewsforjudaism.org/staff**

i) Western propaganda on the Bible by highly reputable Jesus-deniers.

j) Those are extensive and argue that the New Testament contains too many anomalies, but there is no fraud or conspiracy in its publication.

k) Those include books, YouTube videos, podcasts, debates etc. on the truth of the story of Jesus:
   i) By Dr. Bart D. Ehrman: **https://en.wikipedia.org/wiki/Bart_D._Ehrman**
   ii) By Dr. David Skrbina: **https://www.davidskrbina.com/**
   iii) By Derek Lambert of MythVision podcasts: **https://www.youtube.com/@MythVisionPodcast**

l) Did Jesus exist: Yes: by Open Mind: **https://www.bbvaopenmind.com/en/science/scientific-insights/did-jesus-of-nazareth-actually-exist-the-evidence-says-yes/**

***

# Volume 2-Defending the undefendable by Christians

## Volume 2: Ch 6- Babylon is Rome.

### HIGHLIGHTS
* West and Christians are trapped in a lie *
* They had lied and lied that Apostle Peter was crucified by Emperor Nero in the Vatican in 64 AD *
* They have gone too far with the story that he was crucified there upside down *
* But the New Testament claims that Apostle Peter never was in Rome *
* Moreover, Apostle Peter claimed that he was in Babylon in 64 AD *

***New Testament is a lie; Christians knowingly lie to sustain the lie ***
*************************************

1) The West is jointly lying in a conspiracy that Apostle Peter wrote his first epistle from Rome while the Epistle clearly claimed that it was written from Babylon.
2) They argue without any factual basis that Babylon truly meant Rome.
3) This lie is crucial to substantiate another lie: Apostle Peter established the Roman Catholic church before 66 AD.
4) They claim that the Apostle Peter was crucified by Emperor Nero after the infamous fire at Nero's circus in Rome, the Vatican, in 66 AD. (Ref: a, b & c)
5) But the New Testament has another story.
6) Apostle Peter writes in conclusion in chapter 5.

> 1Pe. 5:13    *She who is in **Babylon**, chosen together with you, sends you her greetings, and so does my son Mark.*

> 1Pe. 5:14    *Greet one another with a kiss of love. Peace to all of you who are in Christ.*

7) The Apostle Peter claimed he was in Babylon, not Rome.
8) Apostle Peter never went to Rome.
9) This is quite clear from the New Testament, particularly the Book of Acts.
10) It is impossible for any Jew, Greek, or British to assume that Babylon was Rome in the first century or any time thereafter.
11) Babylon and Rome are very well understood by them.
12) God ordered Abraham to leave Babylon and covet the land of the Canaanites, meaning Israel, as per the Bible's Genesis.
13) All the Gospels mention and identify Babylon many times.
14) Babylon is mentioned eleven times in the New Testament.
15) Rome is mentioned ten times, and the term Roman is mentioned thirteen times.

16) Roman Catholics built so many monuments and basilicas in Rome in honor of the Apostle Peter, establishing a church there and getting crucified there.

17) It was a white lie gone too far to be retrieved.

**18) There is no way to escape other than to lie that Babylon was Rome.**

**19) This lie by the Christians will stand at the gates of Heaven, and God will judge the lie of the British.**


References:

a) Saint Peter; Wikipedia: **https://en.wikipedia.org/wiki/Saint_Peter**

b) What is the evidence that Peter was crucified upside down in Rome: Evidence for Christianity: **https://evidenceforchristianity.org/what-is-the-evidence-that-peter-was-crucified-upside-down-in-rome/**

c) The Crucifixion of St. Peter: **https://www.dulwichpicturegallery.org.uk/explore-the-collection/051-100/the-crucifixion-of-saint-peter/**

d) How did St. Peter die? Britannica: **https://www.britannica.com/question/How-did-St-Peter-die**

e) Videos, debates, and presentations by Rabbi Michel Skobac in Jews for Judaism; **https://jewsforjudaism.org/staff**

f) Western propaganda on the Bible by highly reputable Jesus-deniers.

g) Those are extensive and argue that the New Testament contains too many anomalies, but there is no fraud or conspiracy in its publication.

h) Those include books, YouTube videos, podcasts, debates etc. on the truth of the story of Jesus:

    i) By Dr. Bart D. Ehrman: **https://en.wikipedia.org/wiki/Bart_D._Ehrman**

    ii) By Dr. David Skrbina: **https://www.davidskrbina.com/**

    iii) By Derek Lambert of MythVision podcasts: **https://www.youtube.com/@MythVisionPodcast**

i) Did Jesus exist: Yes: by Open Mind: **https://www.bbvaopenmind.com/en/science/scientific-insights/did-jesus-of-nazareth-actually-exist-the-evidence-says-yes/**

***

## <u>Volume 2-Defending the undefendable by Christians</u>

## <u>Volume 2: Ch 7- Paul is Peter.</u>

### <u>HIGHLIGHTS</u>
* Christians have built the Basilica of St. Peter in the Vatican and collect cash daily *
* The basilica was built to fake that St. Peter established the Roman Catholic Church *
* They invent stories that St. Peter was crucified upside down by Emperor Nero *
* Simultaneously, they invent stories that Emperor Nero beheaded St. Paul in Rome *
* The Bible says that the Apostle Paul established the Roman church *
* The Bible says that St. Peter never set foot in Rome *
* Two basilicas are earning billions: the aim of these stories *
***Christians have no qualms about inventing fake stories to steal cash ***
****************************************

1) The most iconic monument of the Christians is the Basilica of St. Peter in the heart of the Vatican. (Ref: a-f).
2) It is a familiar story invented by Christians that the Apostle Peter was crucified upside down at this very spot in 64 AD. (Ref: a-f).
3) It is a familiar story that the remains of Apostle Peter were excavated from under the church.
4) It is a familiar story that Apostle Peter preached the Gospel to the Romans and thereby established the Roman Catholic Church around 64 AD.
5) This story fulfilled Jesus' words that the Apostle Peter was appointed the "**rock of the church.**"
6) This implied that Apostle Peter would lead the creation of the Christian faith. (Ref: a-f).
7) Based on this, millions of people visit this monument, collecting millions in tourism revenue for the Pope or the Vatican treasury.
8) There is nothing in the New Testament to conclude that Apostle Peter ever visited Rome.
9) In fact, the Book of Acts by Apostle Luke proclaims that Apostle Peter spent the entirety of his ministry in Jerusalem and Judea and converted only circumcised Jews to Christianity there.
10) Apostle Peter also denied the Rome story and declared that Apostle Peter was in Babylon with his family in 64 AD, not Rome.
11) Apostle Peter wrote these verses in his letter titled 1 Peter:

> 1Pe. 5:13    *She who is in **Babylon**, chosen together with you, sends you her greetings, and so does my son Mark.*

> 1Pe. 5:14    *Greet one another with a kiss of love. Peace to all of you who are in Christ.*

12) The same Christians claim that this letter was written in 64-66 AD from Babylon at the same time Apostle Peter was crucified upside down by Roman Emperor Nero in 64-66 AD.

13) Now, Jesus is caught in a dilemma.

14) How do we overcome the death of Apostle Peter in Rome while he was writing letters from Babylon at the same time?

15) All these fake stories and dates were stamped, sealed, and gazetted already.

16) There is only one way: add one more lie.

17) Babylon is Rome.

18) Apostle Peter meant Rome when he wrote Babylon in his own hands.

19) Apostle Peter wrote this with his own hands.

20) Now everyone knows the enormous stories invented by the Christians around a possible fake character, Emperor Nero, in epic movies, novels, and history, at the same time earning big-time cash by the Christians from the new inventions. (Ref: a-f).

21) All these established the falsehood that Apostle Peter established the Roman Catholic church.

22) The most exciting story, but not well deciphered, is that Emperor Nero simultaneously beheaded the Apostle Paul in Rome.

23) Both executions occurred soon after the great fire in Nero's circus. (Ref: a-f).

24) Another epic church, the Basilica of St. Paul in Rome, also eulogizes Apostle Paul.

25) This monument is considered inferior to the Basilica of St. Peter.

26) Millions of people also visit this monument, collecting millions in tourism revenue for the Pope or the Vatican treasury.

27) Though Apostle Peter never touched Rome, as per the New Testament, Apostle Paul, after staying in Rome under house arrest, disappeared into thin air, as per the Book of Acts, purportedly written by Apostle Luke.

28) It was supposed to be "an orderly account" written by Apostle Luke, who was in Rome at the time.

29) The book of Acts, written by Apostle Luke, concluded in great mystery in the last verse of the last chapter:

> Ac. 28:30    *For two whole years Paul stayed there in his own rented house and welcomed all who came to see him.*

> Ac. 28:31    *Boldly and without hindrance he preached the kingdom of God and taught about the Lord Jesus Christ.*

30) You can see that Apostle Luke is very deceptive in concluding the "orderly account" in such great suspense.

31) Apostle Luke, who was in Rome with Apostle Paul for the whole two years, does not mention Apostle Peter in Rome.

32) What is clear, if there is any truth in the New Testament, is that Apostle Luke lived to write the Book of Acts after the mystery end of the Book.

33) He could not have been beheaded by Emperor Nero in 64 AD.

34) Apostle Luke preferred to mesmerize the readers with the mystery end.

35) **The same scholars who vouch that Apostle Paul was beheaded in Rome in 64 AD also claim that Apostle Paul wrote many letters after his unexplained return to Greece after the beheading by Emperor Nero.** (Ref: a-f).

36) In summary, Apostle Peter won first prize in Rome, and Apostle Paul was relegated to second prize by Christians, who preferred Jesus's words to the Word of God.

37) **Christians are still capable of doing miracles like Jesus, crucifying Apostle Peter in Rome while he was in Babylon with his family.**

References:

a) Apostle Peter in Rome: **https://www.biblicalarchaeology.org/daily/ancient-cultures/ancient-rome/the-apostle-peter-in-rome/**

b) Introduction to First Epistle General of Peter: **https://www.churchofjesuschrist.org/study/manual/new-testament-seminary-teacher-manual/introduction-to-the-first-epistle-general-of-peter?lang=eng**

c) St. Peter's Tomb: Wikipedia: **https://en.m.wikipedia.org/wiki/Saint_Peter%27s_tomb**

d) Tradition of Peter in Rome: Britannica: **https://www.britannica.com/biography/Saint-Peter-the-Apostle/Tradition-of-Peter-in-Rome**

e) Basilica of St. John: Wikipedia: **https://en.m.wikipedia.org/wiki/Basilica_of_St._John**

f) The History of St. Peter's Basilica: **https://www.whatalifetours.com/the-history-of-st-peters-basilica/#:~:text=The%20crucifixion%20took%20place%20near,several%20ancient%20Obelisks%20of%20Rome**

g) Videos, debates, and presentations by Rabbi Michel Skobac in Jews for Judaism; **https://jewsforjudaism.org/staff**

h) Western propaganda on the Bible by highly reputable Jesus-deniers.

i) Those are extensive & argue that there are too many anomalies in the New Testament, but there is no fraud or conspiracy in the publication of the New Testament.

j) Those include books, YouTube videos, podcasts, debates etc. on the truth of the story of Jesus:

   i) By Dr. Bart D. Ehrman: **https://en.wikipedia.org/wiki/Bart_D._Ehrman**

   ii) By Dr. David Skrbina: **https://www.davidskrbina.com/**

   iii) By Derek Lambert of MythVision podcasts: **https://www.youtube.com/@MythVisionPodcast**

k) Did Jesus exist: Yes: by Open Mind: **https://www.bbvaopenmind.com/en/science/scientific-insights/did-jesus-of-nazareth-actually-exist-the-evidence-says-yes/**

***

## <u>Volume 2-Defending the undefendable by Christians</u>

## <u>Volume 2: Ch 8- Queen Helina discovers Golgotha</u>

### <u>HIGHLIGHTS</u>
* Romans who crucified Jesus at Golgotha had to invent Golgotha three centuries later *
* To do that, Queen Helena, at the age of 82, sailed from Rome to Israel in 325 AD *
* There was no church in Jerusalem for three centuries after Jesus *
* There was no Christian in Israel for three centuries after Jesus *
*** The story of Jesus is a scam to steal cash from the naïve laity ***
*************************************

1) After inventing Jesus, the British spent millions to build monuments around Europe and in and around the land of Jesus.
2) But it was only a fraction of the weekly Sunday loot after the prayer of confession worldwide.
3) To seal their scam, they installed all kinds of evidence, including Michael Angelo paintings and other incredible monuments.
4) The mastermind of the Gospels had ensured that Golgotha, the hill where Jesus was supposed to have been crucified, and its location remained a total mystery in the Gospel narratives.
5) We should assume that Golgotha never existed.
6) If anything was true in the New Testament, the Romans, Pontius Pilate, and the chief priest of the Sanhedrin knew the precise location of the crucifixion site.
7) They must have recorded it.
8) **The lack of this record proves the scam of the story of Jesus.**
9) And as per the book of Acts, there were five thousand Jesus-believers in Jerusalem soon after the crucifixion of Jesus.
10) Jesus, Son of God, preached and performed miracles to make Jews believe in Jesus, but they crucified him instead of believing in him.
11) But suddenly, Apostle Peter converted three thousand Jews with one speech in one day.
12) If that were true, we should expect a few churches for them to assemble and pray in Jerusalem.
13) But they assembled in temple courts and in Synagogues, which is a lie because the Jews would have thrown them out.
14) We read in the book of Acts, chapter 2:

> *Ac. 2:40     With many other words he warned them; and he pleaded with them, "Save yourselves from this corrupt generation."*

*Ac. 2:41*    **Those who accepted his message were baptised, and about three thousand were added to their number that day.**

*Ac. 2:42*    *They devoted themselves to the apostles' teaching and to the fellowship, to the breaking of bread and to prayer.*

*Ac. 2:43*    *Everyone was filled with awe, and many wonders and miraculous signs were done by the apostles.*

*Ac. 2:44*    *All the believers were together and had everything in common.*

*Ac. 2:45*    *Selling their possessions and goods, they gave to anyone as he had need.*

*Ac. 2:46*    **Every day they continued to meet together in the temple courts.** *They broke bread in their homes and ate together with glad and sincere hearts,*

15) **The proof that no church existed in Jerusalem supports the scam theory**.

16) If the New Testament accounts are true, we should expect at least one hundred thousand Jews to be baptized and become Christians by 50 AD.

17) If we believe it, we should expect at least 10% of Jews to be Christians today in Israel.

18) That would be about a million Christians.

19) Instead, we see just 0.4% as Christians of Jewish origin.

20) That amounts to less than fifty thousand Christians today in Israel.

21) **Again, it supports the scam theory.**

22) The Ivy League scholars have invented another story that establishes that Jerusalem did not have a church until 346 AD. (Ref: a- h)

23) This proved that there were no Christians in Israel until 346 AD.

24) **This again supports the scam theory.**

25) We can easily imagine that sailing from Rome to Jerusalem was a risky venture in those days.

26) The story goes on to say that Romans, who knew where Jesus was crucified, had to send their old and ready-to-die Queen Helena to sail all the way to Israel in her old age to locate Golgotha in 325 AD. (Ref: a- h)

27) She did locate it, as per the current stories.

28) Queen Helena died two years later, in 327 AD.

29) Her son, Constantine the Great, the emperor of Rome, made her do this risky endeavor. (Ref: a- h)

30) Finally, she discovers the place and returns to Rome, where the Emperor, Constantine the Great, gets the first church built in 346 AD.

31) This is called the church of the Holy Sepulcher.

32) Why should a Roman Emperor build this church in Jerusalem in 346 AD?

33) Because there was no Jewish Christians in Jerusalem.

34) Many stories are further invented to claim that a church at that location was built in 1810 with all the evidence of earlier churches and other evidence.

35) With no Christians or very few Christians there in Israel, we should expect that those praying in the churches in Israel are foreign Christians, visiting as tourists.

36) According to publicity, this church was burnt down by a fire, after which a new church was built with all the proof of history. (Ref: a- h)

37) Any reasonable person can figure out that the fire was fake to fake that there was an old church there.

38) This church is not owned by anybody in Israel but by churches elsewhere, including the Roman Catholic Church. (Ref: a- h)

**39) That again supports the scam theory; there is no Christian in Israel to support all these incredible stories.**

40) Foreign Christians have built many such monuments in Israel.

41) Jews are happy to derive all the tourism money from the foreigners visiting this "Holy monument" of the British scam.

**42) Given these incredible and untenable stories, we can conclude that this new church, built in 1810 in Israel by foreigners, was the first monument built in Jerusalem to seal the scam, which the British created around the same time.**

References:


a) Helena, mother of Constantine 1: **https://en.wikipedia.org/wiki/Helena,_mother_of_Constantine_I**

b) St. Helena discovers True Cross (250-350 AD) by A.R. Birley: Try google search.

c) The Garden Tomb: Wikipedia: **https://en.m.wikipedia.org/wiki/The_Garden_Tomb**

d) Calvary: Wikipedia: **https://en.m.wikipedia.org/wiki/The_Garden_Tomb**

e) Golgotha and Temple Mount: **https://www.esv.org/resources/esv-global-study-bible/illustration-43-golgotha/**

f) Golgotha, the place of the skull: Revealed Truth: **https://www.revealedtruth.com/cross/golgotha-skull-hill/**

g) Where is Golgotha? Where Jesus was crucified: **https://www.biblicalarchaeology.org/daily/biblical-sites-places/jerusalem/where-is-golgotha-where-jesus-was-crucified/**

h) Where was Golgotha: Grace Communion: **https://www.gci.org/articles/where-was-golgotha/**

i) Videos, debates, and presentations by Rabbi Michel Skobac in Jews for Judaism; **https://jewsforjudaism.org/staff**

j) Western propaganda on the Bible by highly reputable Jesus-deniers.

k) Those are extensive and argue that the New Testament contains too many anomalies, but there is no fraud or conspiracy in its publication.

l) Those include books, YouTube videos, podcasts, debates etc. on the truth of the story of Jesus:

   i)    By Dr. Bart D. Ehrman: **https://en.wikipedia.org/wiki/Bart_D._Ehrman**

   ii)   By Dr. David Skrbina: **https://www.davidskrbina.com/**

   iii)  By Derek Lambert of MythVision podcasts: **https://www.youtube.com/@MythVisionPodcast**

m) Did Jesus exist: Yes: by Open Mind: **https://www.bbvaopenmind.com/en/science/scientific-insights/did-jesus-of-nazareth-actually-exist-the-evidence-says-yes/**


***

# Volume 2-Defending the undefendable by Christians

## Volume 2: Ch 9- Churches built around the globe.

### HIGHLIGHTS
* The Christians built epic churches after 1400AD to seal the scam *
* They invented evidence to falsify that they were built or rebuilt those churches that were built in the fourth century *
* First, they invented Jesus after 1400 AD and falsified that it was invented in the first century *
* Then they built epic monuments after 1400 AD and falsified that those were built in the fourth century *
*** Scam of Jesus is sealed by the Scam of the churches ***
********************

1) Roman Catholics and Anglicans started a campaign of building monumental churches around the globe after 1500 AD, soon after they invented the story of Jesus.
2) In every case, they claimed that those were built to replace churches built in the fourth century.
3) They provided evidence of the existence of the earlier churches.
4) It was all about making up historical stories that are not traceable or provable, told by the same group of scammers. (See volumes 3, 4 & 5).
5) **The West invented the scam of Jesus and sealed it with the scam of the monument building.**

References:
   a) Videos, debates and presentations by Rabbi Michel Skobac in Jews for Judaism; **https://jewsforjudaism.org/staff**
   b) Western propaganda on the Bible by highly reputable Jesus-deniers.
   c) Those are extensive and argue that the New Testament contains too many anomalies, but there is no fraud or conspiracy in its publication.
   d) Those include books, YouTube videos, podcasts, debates etc. on the truth of the story of Jesus:
       i)     By Dr. Bart D. Ehrman: **https://en.wikipedia.org/wiki/Bart_D._Ehrman**
       ii)     By Dr. David Skrbina: **https://www.davidskrbina.com/**
       iii)     By Derek Lambert of MythVision podcasts: **https://www.youtube.com/@MythVisionPodcast**

   e) Did Jesus exist: Yes: by Open Mind: **https://www.bbvaopenmind.com/en/science/scientific-insights/did-jesus-of-nazareth-actually-exist-the-evidence-says-yes/**

***

## Volume 2-Defending the undefendable by Christians

## Volume 2: Ch 10- Apostle John died in Ephesus.

### HIGHLIGHTS
* The New Testament does not describe the works of Apostle John *
* He is depicted as an assistant to Apostle Peter staying in Jerusalem *
* Apostle John never traveled out of Israel *
* Yet many stories are invented by Christians to prove otherwise *
***The story of Jesus is invented to cheat and win ***
**************************************

1) Christians highly revere Apostle John with millions of invented stories.
2) Many earn big money selling statues of St. John online and offline. (Ref: a-e)
3) The Gospels and the New Testament clearly show that Apostle John is a dubious and unreliable character.
4) Apostle John called himself "**Disciple whom Jesus loved,**" though no other disciples mentioned such a claim.
5) The more unreliable a character is, the more stories Christians invent to eulogize him to distract from the unreliability.
6) Apostle John plays a minimal role in the Era of the Apostles' ministry.
7) In the New Testament, he is depicted as an assistant of Apostle Peter, just standing around when Apostle Peter delivers miraculous deeds in Jerusalem, Judea, soon after Jesus's ascension to heaven.
8) The New Testament does not mention that Apostle John traveled out of Judea, Israel, to eulogize and spread the message of Jesus.
9) In fact, none of the disciples did so except Apostle Paul, who was not one of Jesus's twelve disciples.
10) Yet, Ivy League scholars have invented millions of stories to elevate his status as a Saint. (Ref: a-e)
11) Apostle John is said to have written five of the twenty-seven books of the New Testament.
12) As an escape route, scholars have established another story that the Apostle John may not have written those books.
13) The undisputed position of the scholars is that nothing in the story of Jesus makes sense.
14) Still, the story is true: God sent Jesus to Israel either to rule Jews for eternity or to die on the cross to come again for the final judgment.

15) Stories are invented claiming that Apostle John lived to 95 and died a natural death in the Turkish city of Ephesus.

16) That was to validate the very last chapter of his Gospel.

17) This validates that Apostle John wrote the Gospel of John in 95 AD when he was 95. (Ref: a-e)

18) Roman Emperor Justinian claimed to have built the Basilica of St. John in the sixth century at Ephesus.

19) They claim that this Basilica is in ruins and publish many pictures of the ruins. (Ref: a-e)

20) The pictures speak for themselves; those are fake or deepfake.

21) Within those stories, they claim that Apostle John was banished to live in isolation on Patmos Island, from where he wrote all these five books. (Ref: a-e)

22) That is a self-defeating story.

23) The Apostle John was a fisherman from Galilee who could not write or read, as the New Testament depicts.

24) And writing on scrolls or papyrus was a highly specialized skill of the few.

25) And writing a long book on papyrus in those days was not like making a painting on a rock.

26) The Ivy League scholars had invented a story in which assistants wrote many of the twenty-seven books to overcome this handicap and anomaly.

27) They invent stories with an escape route.

28) But here, Apostle Paul was in isolation with no scrolls and pens to write on.

29) At that time in the first century, no paper existed as paper was first invented in China in the second century AD.(Ref: f, g & h)

30) Apostle John did the impossible in the first century AD.

31) Apostle John wrote in 2 John 12 as follows:

> 2Jn. 12    *I have much to write to you, but **I do not want to use paper and ink**. Instead, I hope to visit you and talk with you face to face, so that our joy may be complete.*

32) He wrote it himself personally:

33) The unschooled Apostle John could write on paper even before paper was invented.

**34) The British have talent!**

**35) To lie and weave the lie beyond comprehension and dispute.**


References:


a) John of Patmos: Wikipedia: **https://en.wikipedia.org/wiki/John_of_Patmos**

b) John the Evangelist: Wikipedia: **https://en.wikipedia.org/wiki/John_of_Patmos**

c) How did Apostle John die? **https://www.biblestudy.org/question/how-did-apostle-john-die.html**

d) Basilica of St. John: **https://ephesus.us/around-ephesus/basilica-of-st-john/**

e) St. John the Apostle: Britannica: **https://www.britannica.com/biography/Saint-John-the-Apostle**

f) History of paper by American Forest & Paper Association: **https://www.afandpa.org/news/2021/history-paper#:~:text=About%202%2C000%20years%20ago%2C%20inventors,Lun%2C%20a%20Chinese%20court%20official.**

g)  Papermaking Process by Brittanica: **https://www.britannica.com/technology/papermaking**
h)  Papermaking by Wikipedia:
**https://en.wikipedia.org/wiki/Papermaking#:~:text=Papermaking%2C%20regardless%20of%20the%20 scale,of%20fibres%20using%20a%20press**.
i)  Videos, debates, and presentations by Rabbi Michel Skobac in Jews for Judaism;
**https://jewsforjudaism.org/staff**
j)  Western propaganda on the Bible by highly reputable Jesus-deniers.
k)  Those are extensive and argue that the New Testament contains too many anomalies, but there is no fraud or conspiracy in its publication.
l)  Those include books, YouTube videos, podcasts, debates etc. on the truth of the story of Jesus:
    i)    By Dr. Bart D. Ehrman: **https://en.wikipedia.org/wiki/Bart_D._Ehrman**
    ii)   By Dr.  David Skrbina:  **https://www.davidskrbina.com/**
    iii)  By Derek Lambert of MythVision podcasts: **https://www.youtube.com/@MythVisionPodcast**

m)  Did Jesus exist: Yes: by Open Mind: **https://www.bbvaopenmind.com/en/science/scientific-insights/did-jesus-of-nazareth-actually-exist-the-evidence-says-yes/**

***

# Volume 2-Defending the undefendable by Christians

## Volume 2: Ch 11- Jesus is not God for Anglican Bishops.

### HIGHLIGHTS
* Anglican bishops in Britain recant the story of Jesus *
* They accept that Jesus is not God but an agent of God *
*The British are slowly accepting their deceit *
*** British invented Jesus to Cheat and Win ***
******************************************

1) Recently, half of the Anglican bishops in Britain declared that it was not necessary to consider that Jesus was God. (Ref: a & b))
2) Instead, they claimed that it was good enough for Christians to accept that Jesus is the "God's supreme agent."
3) It is a total rejection of the New Testament.
4) And therefore, an admission that the New Testament is a scam.
5) It is a way to keep the funds coming from the laity sustaining the scam of Jesus.
6) We are witnessing a gradual erosion of the New Testament within the church.
7) Those who profess that we should treat the New Testament as the Word of God and that we should not change even a letter are fast losing ground to the liberals.
8) The conservatives are clear: if we do not give way to some of these liberal views, our jobs, income, and livelihoods will be lost.
9) We are getting closer and closer to the ultimate truth that materialism is the root of Jesus's godliness.
10) All these lead us to the ultimate truth: Jesus did not exist, and the British invented Jesus to cheat and win after 1492 AD.

References:

a) Anglican bishops declare that Jesus is not God: **https://www.answering-christianity.com/ac/ang.htm**
b) Praying to "Our Father" is problematic: Fox News: **https://www.foxnews.com/media/anglican-archbishop-declares-father-problematic-oppressively-patriarchal**
c) A letter in response to the Bishop of Oxford: Joshua Penduck: **https://www.fulcrum-anglican.org.uk/articles/a-letter-in-response-to-the-bishop-of-oxford/**
d) Videos, debates, and presentations by Rabbi Michel Skobac in Jews for Judaism; **https://jewsforjudaism.org/staff**
e) Western propaganda on the Bible by highly reputable Jesus-deniers.

f) Those are extensive and argue that the New Testament contains too many anomalies, but there is no fraud or conspiracy in its publication.

g) Those include books, YouTube videos, podcasts, debates etc. on the truth of the story of Jesus:

    i)      By Dr. Bart D. Ehrman: **https://en.wikipedia.org/wiki/Bart_D._Ehrman**

    ii)     By Dr. David Skrbina: **https://www.davidskrbina.com/**

    iii)    By Derek Lambert of MythVision podcasts: **https://www.youtube.com/@MythVisionPodcast**

h) Did Jesus exist: Yes: by Open Mind: **https://www.bbvaopenmind.com/en/science/scientific-insights/did-jesus-of-nazareth-actually-exist-the-evidence-says-yes/**

***

## Volume 2-Defending the undefendable by Christians

## Volume 2: Ch 12- I am Holy, you are a Cheater.

### HIGHLIGHTS
* The British had created the White Supremacy theory in the world *
* They used the story of Jesus to create that theory *
*** Jesus was mixed with TripleSin ***
********************

1) The British effectively used "divide and rule" to manage the TripleSin.
2) They used religions and beliefs to divide people.
3) They created a belief that the British were a superior race with a true God always on their side.
4) "All of you are pagans and cheaters; we are holy": that sums up the illusion created.
5) Even today, many victims believe that the Triple-sinners reformed the world while Triple-sinning.
6) Many believe that they dismantled slavery in Asia while their brothers were selling seventeen-year-old African girls as slaves, not one or two, but millions in the new Christian land, the Americas.
7) The pope and Archbishop joined the rest in churches globally to pray to Jesus to bless their trade.
8) Now, the British have become the USA or the Americans.
9) They use the same theology:
   "All of you are pagans and cheaters; we are holy."
10) Americans sang to the world: "Cubans, Russians, and Chinese are godless evil people, and Africans are monkeys," but we are Saints.
11) They jointly expanded their Christian Caliphate, nicknamed NATO.
12) and shamelessly claim they are defending freedom, the same game with a new slogan.
13) Anyone not supporting the Christian Caliphate is terrorist and anti-democratic.
14) By this double game, they invade the land of others by proxy wars.
15) Indians were longtime allies until India refused to gang up with the new oil sanction of the Christian mafia, ***fixing the price of your oil and my oil***.
16) Suddenly, India is pro-Hindu and anti-Muslim.
17) There is no religious freedom in India.
18) Suddenly, Adani adopts "our Wall Street game," blessed by Jesus, and manipulates the price of Wall Street.

19) "**Jesus is the Son of True God**" is the name of the game — the giant money-laundering game.


References:


a)  Arrogant British: The Telegraph: **https://www.telegraph.co.uk/travel/736311/Arrogant-unfriendly-and-no-sense-of-humour-what-foreign-tourists-think-of-the-English.html**

b)  French is arrogant: The Telegraph: **https://www.telegraph.co.uk/news/worldnews/europe/eu/10055933/British-say-the-French-are-the-most-arrogant-people-in-Europe-and-the-French-agree.html**

c)  Churchill a Racist: Daily Mail: **https://www.dailymail.co.uk/news/article-12230369/Anger-Winston-Churchills-family-St-Pauls-Cathedral-lambasts-white-supremacist.html**

d)  Videos, debates, and presentations by Rabbi Michel Skobac in Jews for Judaism; **https://jewsforjudaism.org/staff**

e)  Western propaganda on the Bible by highly reputable Jesus-deniers.

f)  Those are extensive and argue that the New Testament contains too many anomalies, but there is no fraud or conspiracy in its publication.

g)  Those include books, YouTube videos, podcasts, debates etc. on the truth of the story of Jesus:

   i)  By Dr. Bart D. Ehrman: **https://en.wikipedia.org/wiki/Bart_D._Ehrman**

   ii)  By Dr. David Skrbina: **https://www.davidskrbina.com/**

   iii)  By Derek Lambert of MythVision podcasts: **https://www.youtube.com/@MythVisionPodcast**

h)  Did Jesus exist: Yes: by Open Mind: **https://www.bbvaopenmind.com/en/science/scientific-insights/did-jesus-of-nazareth-actually-exist-the-evidence-says-yes/**


***

Volume 3

# BUILDING MONUMENTS TO SEAL THE SCAM OF JESUS-JERUSALEM-ISRAEL

# Volume 3- Building Monuments to Seal the Scam of Jesus- (Israel)

# Volume 3- The Monuments and the Cash Cows in Jerusalem, Israel

### HIGHLIGHTS
* Christians invested in monuments to validate the scam of the story of Jesus *
* They invented stories without proper coordination *
* The Lies of Jesus are sustained by more lies by Christians *
*** Church is all about gaining wealth and prestige ***
*****************************************

1) All significant monuments built in Jerusalem to validate the story of Jesus in Israel were built by foreigners and foreign churches, mainly from Rome.
2) Jews or Jewish Christians built none of them.
3) There are not enough Jewish Christians in Jerusalem to build any of those.
4) Foreigners invented the story of Jesus after 1492 AD.
5) Foreigners invested money earned in the churches to build these monuments after 1492.
6) The common theme is that all those are rebuilt on the remains of the old monument built in the third century AD.
7) That theme is another scam.
8) The British invented the story of Jesus after 1492 AD, faking that it happened in the first century AD.
9) The Roman Catholic Church of the Vatican built the monuments after 1492 AD, faking that they were built on the ruins of those built in the third century.
10) Those churches built by Romans were the first churches in Israel.
11) **The fake claim proved the scam of the story of Jesus because the claim implied that there were no churches in Jerusalem until the third century AD.**
12) All those monuments, mainly called basilicas, are cash cows, as they collect millions daily from Christian tourists who visit and pray there and leave donations.
13) **The scam of monument building is beyond defense.**

References:
a) Who Built Jerusalem: Saint Helena: **https://www.steinbergtourguide.com/post/women-who-built-jerusalem-saint-helena**
b) Churches in Israel: **https://www.beinharimtours.com/churches-in-israel/**
c) Church of the Holy Sepulchre: Wikipedia: **https://en.wikipedia.org/wiki/Church_of_the_Holy_Sepulchre**
d) List of Cathedrals in Israel: **https://en.wikipedia.org/wiki/List_of_cathedrals_in_Israel**
e) Videos, debates and presentations by Rabbi Michel Skobac in Jews for Judaism; **https://jewsforjudaism.org/staff**
f) Western propaganda on the Bible by highly reputable Jesus-deniers.

g) Those are extensive and argue that the New Testament contains too many anomalies, but there is no fraud or conspiracy in its publication.

h) Those include books, YouTube videos, podcasts, debates etc. on the truth of the story of Jesus:

    i)      By Dr. Bart D. Ehrman: **https://en.wikipedia.org/wiki/Bart_D._Ehrman**

    ii)      By Dr. David Skrbina: **https://www.davidskrbina.com/**

    iii)      By Derek Lambert of MythVision podcasts: **https://www.youtube.com/@MythVisionPodcast**

i) Did Jesus exist: Yes: by Open Mind: **https://www.bbvaopenmind.com/en/science/scientific-insights/did-jesus-of-nazareth-actually-exist-the-evidence-says-yes/**

***

# <u>Christian Monuments in Jerusalem in Israel</u>

The New Testament Mastermind who invented the story of Jesus had made several vital locations around Jerusalem **mysterious and unidentifiable**.

1) Golgotha, or Skull Hill, where Jesus was crucified and buried
2) The house where Jesus had the Last Supper
3) The place from where Jesus ascended to heaven
4) The place called Bethany, where Jesus slept while in Jerusalem

The Ivy League scholars, acting as Bible scholars, have invented stories to identify them. Many stories claim that Queen Helena, aged 82 at the time, traveled from Rome to Jerusalem in 325 AD and located them. Most stories claim that Queen Helena only identified Golgotha, where Jesus was crucified.

A careful study would indicate that the scholars' story-making expedition was uncoordinated, resulting in many contradictory claims.

The Mastermind had to amend the story in the Gospel of John that Jesus and his disciples did not walk up to Mount of Olives at midnight or early morning of Good Friday after the Last Supper but walked straight to the garden of Gethsemane.

That version contradicted all three synoptic Gospels, which clearly recorded that Jesus and the disciples walked up the Mount of Olives, prayed there, and then walked down to the garden of Gethsemane, where Jesus again prayed three times before being arrested.

**The Mastermind was forced to lie by amending the story to make it viable, as the time to travel as depicted had made the story of Jesus a hoax.**

The same scholars identified Bethany as Al-Eizaria. Google Maps shows it is at least twelve (12) kilometers from Jerusalem, even after ignoring the elevations. Yet, knowing the accurate distance, scholars and the internet repeatedly claim that it is only three kilometers.

**They are forced to lie since the New Testament explicitly claims so in a deceptive attempt to validate the events that unfolded in Jesus's last days.**

**IVY LEAGUE SCHOLARS ARE DESPERATE TO VOUCH FOR THE LIES OF JESUS**

+++

### Queen Helena built Jerusalem- Hoax to cement Hoax.

The story that Queen Helena, at 82, traveled to Jerusalem from Rome in AD325 in a perilous voyage those days ought to be a scam, as Romans and Jewish priests (Sanhedrin) would have known these locations if the story of Jesus was true.

While the main story says that she discovered Golgotha, the hill where Jesus was crucified, many more stories claim that she found the three crosses; she identified the place Jesus was born in a manger in Bethlehem; she identified where Jesus prayed on top of the Mount of Olives and "place of Abraham" (Mamre Church of Hebron).

With such wild stories, Christians have claimed that his son, Emperor Constantine 1, ordered the building of churches and monuments in the locations around 327 AD.
**(https://www.steinbergtourguide.com/post/women-who-built-jerusalem-saint-helena )**
**( https://www.beinharimtours.com/chapel-of-saint-helena/ )**
**(https://holylandviptours.net/attractions/mamre-a-tribute-to-the-abrahamic/ )**

# <u>Christian Monuments in Jerusalem in Israel-1</u>

## <u>One Church: Many stories</u>
## <u>Basilica of the Holy Sepulcher</u>

(Built in the fourth century AD by Roman Emperor Constantine the Great, but truly built only in 1868 AD by the Roman Catholic Church. As a custom, the scam is that the original church was destroyed in a fire: a convenient way to manipulate history)

(This was built in 1868 AD)

( https://en.wikipedia.org/wiki/Church_of_the_Holy_Sepulchre )

(This was built in 1810 AD)

( https://www.britannica.com/place/Holy-Sepulchre )

(This was built on July 15, 1149 AD)

(https://churchoftheholysepulchre.net/ )

(This was built in 1048 AD)

(https://www.jacksonsun.com/story/news/local/2018/03/23/golgotha-and-church-holy-sepulchre/452788002/ )

# Christian Monuments in Jerusalem in Israel-2

## One Church: Many stories

### Cenacle (Dining Room) @ Last Supper where Jesus had the Last Supper

(Built in between 379-381 AD by Roman Emperor Theodosius 1, but truly built recently by the Roman Catholic church. How and who located this place is not published by the Christians.)

(This was built in 1831 AD)

(https://en.wikipedia.org/wiki/Cenacle#:~:text=The%20Cenacle%20(from%20the%20Latin,meal%20that%2C%20in%20the%20Gospel )

(There is no record of who built this fancy modern building, but it makes a lot of tourist money)

( https://www.itraveljerusalem.com/attraction/the-last-supper-room )

(This was built after the sixteenth century)

( https://www.historyhit.com/locations/the-coenaculum-jerusalem/ )

# <u>Christian Monuments in Jerusalem in Israel-3</u>

<u>One Church: Many stories</u>

<u>Church of Nativity, where Jesus was born</u>

(Built in the fourth century AD by Roman Emperor Constantine the Great, but truly built only in 1852 AD by the Roman Catholic Church. As a custom, the scam is that invaders destroyed the original church: a convenient way to manipulate history)

(This was built in 1852 AD)

( https://en.wikipedia.org/wiki/Church_of_the_Nativity )

(This was built in "the 19th to 20th centuries, as per UNESCO)

( https://whc.unesco.org/en/list/1433/ )

(It was built in the 12th century, as per Britannica)

( https://www.britannica.com/place/Church-of-the-Nativity )

# <u>Christian Monuments in Jerusalem in Israel-4</u>

## <u>One Church: Many stories</u>
## <u>Chapel of Ascension, from where Jesus ascended to heaven</u>

(Built in the fourth century AD by Roman Emperor Constantine the Great, but truly built only in 1835 AD by the Roman Catholic Church. As a custom, the scam is that invaders destroyed the original church: a convenient way to manipulate history)

(The current chapel was built in 1150 AD; but was initially built around 390 AD by "Poimenia, a wealthy and pious Roman aristocratic woman from the imperial family who financed the building of this chapel")
( https://en.wikipedia.org/wiki/Chapel_of_the_Ascension,_Jerusalem )

(This was built in 1835 AD; it was initially built at the end of the 4th century after Queen Helena established this site)
( https://www.beinharimtours.com/the-church-of-ascension/#:~:text=The%20Chapel%20of%20Ascension,columns%20and%20an%20open%20roof. )

(Fake Footstep of Jesus on the Church of Ascension)
(https://www.jpost.com/arab-israeli-conflict/in-jesuss-last-footsteps-453194 )

# Christian Monuments in Jerusalem in Israel-5

### One Church: Many stories
### The Chapel of Ascension, from where Jesus ascended to heaven, was built by the Russian Orthodox Church in the 1870s

(The current chapel was built in 1870 AD)

(Incredibly, this church was built on the Mount of Olives by the Russian Orthodox Church and contains the head of John the Baptist)

( https://www.seetheholyland.net/wp-content/uploads/Hollow-in-floor-where-John-the-Baptists-head-is-believed-to-have-been-found-Matanya-Wikimedia--225x300.jpg )

THIS IS TRULY INCREDIBLE AS JOHN THE BAPTIST'S HEAD WAS GIVEN TO HERODIAS, WIFE OF HEROD ANTIPAS, IN 30 AD IN GALILEE, 200 KILOMETERS NORTH OF JERUSALEM AND THE MOUNT OF OLIVES

+++

Volume 4


# BUILDING MONUMENTS TO SEAL THE SCAM OF JESUS-ROME-ITALY

# Volume 4-Building Monuments to Seal the Scam of Jesus (Vatican)

## Volume 4: The Monuments, the Cash Cows, of Vatican, Rome

### HIGHLIGHTS
* Christians jointly invented Jesus and concurrently invented TripleSin *
* Christians prayed to Jesus to bless them, and Jusus readily complied *
* The Christian Golden Era arrived *
* And Christians invested all the money in building monuments to validate the scam of Jesus *
*** Church is all about gaining wealth and prestige ***
****************************************

1) The most significant money laundering scheme ever is the TripleSin (Slave Trade, colonialism, and Apartheid) run by the Western Christians.
2) TripleSin was run jointly by the Western Countries led by the British.
3) The British invented the story of Jesus in the New Testament after 1498 AD, as solidly established in the book "**British Invented Jesus to Cheat and Win.**"
4) With all the money stolen from the East by the TripleSin, the Christians built monuments worldwide after 1600 AD, eulogizing either Mother Mary or the disciples, but not Jesus.
5) The scam of Jesus' story was founded on the disciples and their witness testimony.
6) The bonanza of building monuments was a planned investment to seal the scam and keep the money flowing.
7) We can see the game of scammers in pictures of the monuments and by analyzing the facts and claims provided by the scammers in the Western world.
8) There are three salient points to focus on when we analyze them.
9) The first point is the contradictions of the stories, as there was no central control in the game.
10) In TripleSinning and colonization, the British fought Italians, and Portuguese.
11) In the scam of Jesus, they invented their preferred stories.
12) The second point is that scammers were going around the world, building these monuments to seal and validate the stories they invented as they occurred in those foreign lands.
13) Jews did not build any Christian monuments in Israel, but Romans did.
14) Greeks did not build Christian monuments in Greece, but Romans did.
15) Turks built no Christian monuments in Turkey, but Romans did.
16) Indians did not build Christian monuments in India, but the Portuguese did first in regions where they had control, and then the British did in areas where they got control.
17) The third point is a common lie.

18) To seal Jesus's scam, they uniformly published a fake claim that they were all built after 1600 AD in places where monuments were earlier built in the first four centuries AD.
19) **The scam of monument building is beyond defense.**

References:

a) Basilicas of Catholic Church:
**https://en.m.wikipedia.org/wiki/Basilicas_in_the_Catholic_Church#Minor_basilicas**

b) Seven Pilgrim Churches of Rome: Wikipedia:
**https://en.wikipedia.org/wiki/Seven_Pilgrim_Churches_of_Rome**

c) Top Ten churches to visit in Rome: **https://www.pnac.org/visitorsoffice/top-ten-churches-to-visit-in-rome/**

d) The Four Major Basilicas in Rome: **https://carpediemtours.com/blog/four-major-basilicas-rome/**

e) Videos, debates, and presentations by Rabbi Michel Skobac in Jews for Judaism;
**https://jewsforjudaism.org/staff**

f) Western propaganda on the Bible by highly reputable Jesus-deniers.

g) Those are extensive and argue that the New Testament contains too many anomalies, but there is no fraud or conspiracy in its publication.

h) Those include books, YouTube videos, podcasts, debates etc., on the truth of the story of Jesus:

   i) By Dr. Bart D. Ehrman: **https://en.wikipedia.org/wiki/Bart_D._Ehrman**

   ii) By Dr. David Skrbina: **https://www.davidskrbina.com/**

   iii) By Derek Lambert of MythVision podcasts: **https://www.youtube.com/@MythVisionPodcast**

i) Did Jesus exist: Yes: by Open Mind: **https://www.bbvaopenmind.com/en/science/scientific-insights/did-jesus-of-nazareth-actually-exist-the-evidence-says-yes/**

***

# <u>Vatican Monuments in Italy-1</u>

### <u>St. Peter's Basilica in the Vatican</u>

(Built in honor of Apostle Peter, who was crucified in Rome by Emperor Nero and who had never been to Rome as per the Bible)

## <u>This was truly built in 1626 AD but faked as built in the fourth century AD</u>

This monument was proudly built on money earned by TripleSin of the West.

Now, it is a cash cow for the Catholics, with millions of tourists donating cash daily.

Built with fake evidence, Apostle Peter, who never set foot in Rome, was crucified on the spot by Emperor Nero in 66 AD, as per the fake stories.

It was built only in 1626 AD, based on a false claim that Emperor Constantine the Great had built a church or monument at this spot in memory of Apostle Peter in the fourth century AD.

(Ref: **https://en.m.wikipedia.org/wiki/St._Peter%27s_Basilica** )

+++

# <u>Vatican Monuments in Italy-2</u>

## <u>St. Paul's Basilica in the Vatican</u>

(Built in honor of Apostle Peter, who was beheaded in Rome by Emperor Nero and who had returned to Greece from the alleged house arrest (and alleged his beheading) in Rome as per the Bible)

### <u>This was truly built in 1825 AD but faked as built in the fourth century AD</u>

This monument was proudly built on money earned by TripleSin of the West.
Now, it is a cash cow for the Catholics, with millions of tourists donating cash daily.

Built with fake evidence, Apostle Paul was beheaded on the spot by Emperor Nero in 65 AD, which contradicted the Bible. As per the Bible, Apostle Paul returned to Greece and wrote many epistles after his return around 65 AD.
It was built only in 1825 AD, based on a false claim that Emperor Constantine the Great had built a church or monument at this spot in memory of Apostle Paul in the fourth century AD.
( Ref: **https://en.m.wikipedia.org/wiki/Basilica_of_Saint_Paul_Outside_the_Walls** )

+++

# Vatican Monuments in Italy-3

## Santa Maria Maggiore
(Built in honor of Mother Mary)

### This was truly built in 1626 AD but faked as built in the fourth century AD

Nothing was built for Jesus in Rome, but they constructed first for Apostle Peter, then for Apostle Paul, and only then for Mother Mary, as per the fake stories of the Christians.

All these stories and monuments were invented after 1492 AD, as evidenced in the book "British Invented Jesus to Cheat and Win."

( Ref: **https://en.wikipedia.org/wiki/Santa_Maria_Maggiore** )

Jesus and the Cross are absent in this church, proving that Jesus was not the church's focus before the New Testament was written after 1492 AD, possibly in 1700 AD.

+++

Volume 5

# FALSIFYING HISTORY BY CHRISTIANS
# KERALA-SOUTH INDIA

# Volume 5-Fabricating History by Christians-Kerala, South India

## Volume 5: Basilica of Malayatoor in Kerala; Wild Stories of Apostle Thomas.

### HIGHLIGHTS
* Epic footprint is destroyed and replaced with man-made replica *
* The giant footprint on the solid rock was that of Apostle Thomas *
* Apostle Thomas prayed there in 64 AD *
* The church built on this false story has become a cash cow *
***A Study and Research on the Story of Jesus is a necessity***
**************************************

1) The making of an unnatural giant footprint, depicted as that of Apostle Paul, on the Malayattoor hilltop around 1500 AD by the then-Jesus-believers and the breaking and obliterating of the unnatural giant footprint around 2000 AD by the current Jesus-believers is a classical reminder of the truth known to the Jesus-believers: that the story of Jesus is a scam benefitting their pockets daily.
2) Strangely, there was only one footprint.
3) The giant footprint was sculptured into the solid granite rock with incredible difficulty.
4) It was double the size of the footprint of any human.
5) The then Jesus-believers must have imagined that Apostle Thomas was a giant.
6) The current Jesus-believers did not want to expose their trickery.
7) They managed to destroy this epic miracle and installed a manmade replica of the miracle.
8) Now, two regular-sized footprints were preserved in a glass enclosure for Jesus-believers to marvel at.
9) And there is an extra miracle now. There is a knee print of Apostle Thomas praying there, kneeling.
10) Christians have invented many stories and built many monuments worldwide to seal and stamp the scam of the New Testament (V3 & V4).
11) We have seen the wild stories made about Apostle John writing epistles in Ephesus (V2 Ch 10).
12) We have seen wild stories made about Apostle Peter and Apostle John in the chapters titled "Paul is Peter" and in "Baylon is Rome" (V2 Ch6 & 7).
13) The Christian plot is to establish that the Apostles went around the world and set up many churches after converting people into believing in Jesus in the first century AD.
14) They built many monuments after 1500 AD, falsely depicting those as made in the first century AD or thereabouts.
15) And they all have become cash cows for the churches.

16) The Book of Acts in the Bible records all the acts of the twelve disciples of Jesus until 66 AD.

17) This book mentions only the acts and deeds of Apostle Peter in Judea.

18) The book does not mention anything done by the rest of the twelve, remembering that Apostle Paul was not one of the twelve disciples.

19) Apostle Thomas is famously known as **Doubting Thomas**.

20) That name came about only because Apostle Thomas doubted the resurrection of Jesus until he inserted his fingers into the nail holes on the hands of Jesus due to the crucifixion.

21) That story was invented to establish that people must blindly believe in Jesus without seeking proof.

22) The character of Apostle Thomas was conceived and fabricated only for that purpose.

23) Nothing is mentioned about Apostle Thomas after the resurrection of Jesus.

24) But we now have many stories and monuments to establish that Apostle Thomas went to Kerala in South India and established a church or many churches there before 64 AD.

25) One story states that the Portuguese discovered this place in 1510 AD, implying that nothing existed there before or that nobody knew about this place.

26) In Those times, South India was a big jungle with a few habitations near the coastal areas.

27) Those jungles were inaccessible and dangerous, with wild animals like tigers, wild boars, and elephants roaming supreme.

28) As per the stories, Apostle Thomas was killed by local Indians in a place called Mylapur in Tamil Nadu in South India (Ref: b).

29) One story stands out.

30) Apostle Thomas went all the way, some 20 kilometers deep into the jungle at Malayattoor hilltop, 609 meters high, and prayed there (ref: a, b, c, and d).

31) The current church at this location attracts a million people to attend mass on Good Fridays yearly (Ref: c).

32) This monument has become a tourist cash cow and a cash cow for the church.

**33) This represents eternal motivation: collecting and pocketing cash from Jesus's Believers.**

References:

a) Malayattoor church: by Diocese: **http://www.ernakulamarchdiocese.org/home/parish/391** )

b) Malayattoor Church: Wikipedia: **https://en.wikipedia.org/wiki/St._Thomas_Syro-Malabar_Church,_Malayattoor)**

c) Peace Healing at Malayattoor Church: **https://www.indiancatholicmatters.org/following-st-thomas-malayattoorr-beckons-pilgrims-to-find-peace-healing/**

d) Pope and Catholic churches in Kerala: **https://www.catholicnewsagency.com/amp/news/36979/pope-praises-beautiful-complex-diversity-of-catholic-churches-in-india**

***

## <u>The current church in 2024 at Malayattoor Hill in Kerala, South India</u>

## THE CONDUCT OF FORGERY BY CHRISTIANS

According to long-held beliefs and stories, Apostle Thomas built a church in the first century AD or that Apostle Thomas prayed at this hilltop in the first century. Both are wild stories. They claim further that the Portuguese discovered this church in 1501 AD.

The hill, at a height of 609 meters, would have been totally inaccessible in the first century AD as it was surrounded by thick forests with tigers, wild boars, and elephants, at least 10 kilometers all around. Even further, Apostle Thomas had no reason to be anywhere around this hill.

(Ref: **https://en.wikipedia.org/wiki/St._Thomas_Syro-Malabar_Church,_Malayattoor**)

The Archdiocese of Ernakulam-Angamaly, which manages this church, does not make such a claim now, having realized the impossibility of these false stories.

(Ref: **http://www.ernakulamarchdiocese.org/home/parish/391** )

## <u>The footprint of Apostle Thomas at the hill of Malayattoor, Kerala, South India</u>

A first look at this giant footprint would expose the forgery.
It was double the size of any human footprint.
There was only one footprint.
This was created to falsify that the Apostle Thomas came to Kerala and established
Christianity in Kerala, South India in the first century AD.

A giant footprint on the solid rock which was the footprint of Apostle Thomas as made out by Christians to
justify the story for centuries was destroyed by the clergy and replaced by a replica within the church
after 1980.
It is not an easy job to destroy the footprint forged by Christians on solid rock.

Now there are two footprints of normal size.
Still, they retain the fraud of the long-held belief with this "man-made" replica.

(Ref: **https://en.wikipedia.org/wiki/St._Thomas_Syro-Malabar_Church,_Malayattoor** )

# Jesus' Dilemma: Jews are Greeks, Babylon is Rome, Paul is Peter

## The Clergy of Fraud and fabrication

The current organization running the Malayattoor church does not seem to claim that Apostle Thomas prayed at the top of the hill in the first century AD because they know that it is an absurd claim.

But they replaced it with a believable replica.
And the cash collections and prayers go on.
(reference: **http://www.ernakulamarchdiocese.org/home/parish/391** )

## Map of Kerala, South India

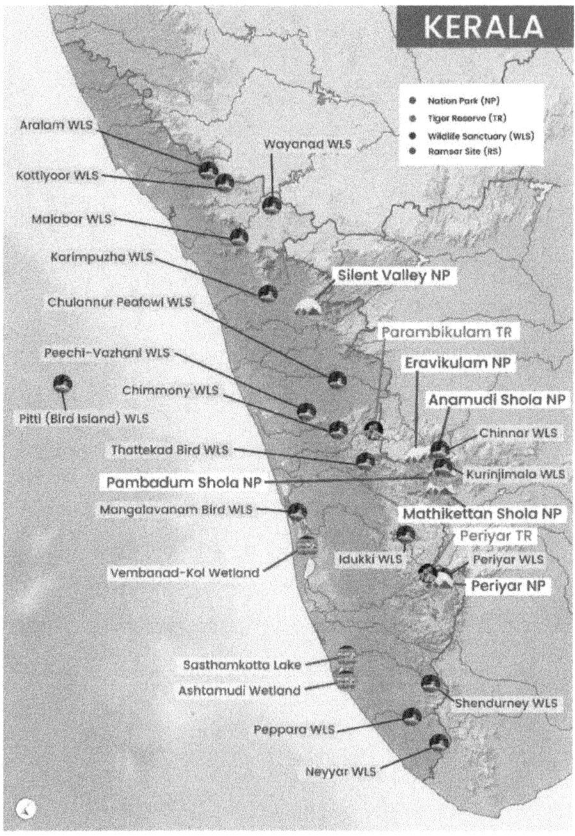


Even today, with more than 34 million people, most hilly areas away from the Coast are wildlife sanctuaries, as seen above.

In the 1900 AD, most places were inaccessible except by boats or on horseback, and wild animals lurked.

In the first century AD, it would have been impossible to go anywhere near Malayattoor, deep in the thick forests of the Western Ghats or Nilageri Hills, known as Sahyaparvatham (Sahya Mountains)

Volume 6

# THE ULTIMATE TRUTH

## <u>Volume 6- The Ultimate Truth</u>

This Volume 6 is a copy of Volume 2G, Chapter 1, published in the book "**British Invented Jesus to Cheat and Win.**"

(volume numbers and chapter numbers are amended here to avoid confusion)

## Volume 6 (2G)-Understanding Jesus (The Ultimate Truth)

## Volume 6 (2G): Ch 1- The Ultimate Truth

### HIGHLIGHTS
* A British Mastermind wrote the New Testament using Greeks *
* They wrote it in Greek while pretending as several Jewish Apostles *
* They wrote it as though it was written before 100 AD *
* The words "to this day" in the Gospel of Matthew exposed that it was written after 300-500 AD *
* The words used by Jesus and later by the Apostles: "church" and "baptism," proved that the New Testament was written after 500 AD *
* The use of the word "paper" in 2 John 12 exposed that the New Testament was written after 1200-1400 AD *
* Finally, the word "Spain" twice used by Apostle Paul in the Epistle to Romans exposed the truth that the New Testament was written originally after 1492 *
* The demotion of Mother Mary and the promotion of Jesus by the Anglican church proved the ultimate truth that the British invented the New Testament with a new story of Jesus after 1600 AD *
*** The Story of Jesus was invented to cheat and gain ***
****************************************

1. The current belief and perception are that the New Testament, particularly the Gospels, was written by living Apostles in the first century AD.
2. Each of the 27 books intentionally creates that belief and impression.
3. The story of Jesus is rooted entirely in that belief and perception.
4. We should not expect that **the word of God** is a scam written to deceive the readers and the believers.
5. We should expect that God's word is perfect, with no anomalies, errors, lies, or slip-ups.
6. But facts in the very narrative of the New Testament prove that a mastermind concocted the story of Jesus with premeditation and wrote it well after 1492 AD, pretending as though several characters, solely to deceive the readers and believers.
7. Summarizing the crucial facts proving this epic deception of inventing a God is good.
8. John the Baptist could not have baptized Jews when baptism was a word to enroll someone since Christians did not exist until centuries later.
9. John the Baptist exhibited an "impossible amnesia" of forgetting who Jesus was *(V2B. Ch 9)*.
10. We have established that Jesus, his disciples, any of the Jewish characters in the New Testament, and the mastermind writing the story were not Jews, but most likely, Greeks because of the "impossible" use of spices in the burial process *(V2B. Ch 15)*.
11. The current Jesus-believers admit that each of all the 27 books in the New Testament was originally written in Greek, meant for Jews, and written by illiterate Apostles: all Jews.
12. They, the scammers, claim that they have these originals.
13. The extensive copycatting and other pretensions in the New Testament establish that the whole of the New Testament was concocted by a mastermind, possibly a British man, who acted as several characters *(V5 Ch 1)*.
14. We have established that Jesus and the Gospel writers consistently misrepresented or amended the verses in the Old Testament to mislead the readers and make them believe that the story of Jesus was prophesized in the Old Testament *(V4. Ch 1)*.

15. We have established initially that Apostle John is a very suspicious character by his own words and his conduct, mainly by:
    a) By his "impossible amnesia" of forgetting who true Jesus was (*V2B. Ch 9*).
    b) By neglecting the crucial role played by his mother (*V2B. Ch 10*).
    c) By his impossible missing of Transfiguration in his Gospel (*V2B. Ch 10*).
    d) By his invention of raising Lazarus from the dead in his Gospel, missing in all three synoptic Gospels, solely to validate the burial of Jesus by leaving in a large open cave (*V2B. Ch 10*).

16. Finally, the late addition of chapter 21 and the narratives in the chapter in the Gospel of John proved and exposed that the writer (the mastermind) was pretending to be Apostle John or a "**disciple whom Jesus loved**" writing. At the same time, he was still alive (*V2B. Ch 12*).

17. Therefore, we know that many disciples did not write the Gospels and the epistles.

18. Additionally, we have established that any of the incidents, starting with the Hosanna procession to the ascension of Jesus to heaven in the final weeks of Jesus' life, could not have occurred by the very descriptions of the narratives, mainly due to the distances and time taken to travel between Jerusalem and the Mount of Olives & Jerusalem and Bethany (*V2C. Ch 1-9*).

19. Having realized the blunder, the Gospel writers tried to salvage it by making the distances shorter by lying; **two lies are in the Gospel of John, and another lie in the Book of Acts** (*V2B. Ch. 2 & V2C. Ch 2 & 7*).

20. Having realized the blunder of the spices used in the burial process in all four Gospels, **Apostle John lied that "this was according to Jewish Customs for burial"** (*V2B. Ch: 15*).

21. Now we establish how the mastermind, by his own words and his unconscious "slip-ups" in his words, exposed that the New Testament was not written in the first century AD but only after 1200-1400 AD.

22. We have seen that by using the words "to this day" and "to this very day" in the Gospel of Matthew, we established that the Gospels and, therefore, the whole of the New Testament was written not before 300-500 AD (*V2B. Ch 18*).

23. Jesus used the word "church", which did not exist until many centuries later (*V2B. Ch 17*).

24. Jesus used the words "baptize" when such a process and such a word did not exist (*V2B. Ch 17*).

25. The words "baptism" and church" go together. People of other faiths get baptized, get converted to Christianity, and then assembled in a church to pray to Jesus.

26. Jesus never went to a church but constantly went to synagogues, even in the last days of his life, proving that church or the concept of church did not exist at those times.

27. Even after Jesus ascended to heaven, the disciples did not assemble in a church and pray; they went upstairs to a house and prayed in a room (*Act 1: 13 & 14*).

28. Apostle Paul used the word "Spain" twice in the Epistle to Romans when such a word or the country "Spain" did not exist until 1492 (*V2D Ch 8*).

29. To cap it all, the word "paper" supposedly used or proposed to be used by the "unschooled" Apostle John in 2 John 12 exposed the ultimate truth of the story of Jesus:

since paper or the word "paper" did not exist in the Middle East until 1200 AD (*V2D. Ch 13*).

30. And such a word did not exist anywhere in the world before 200 AD.
31. Therefore, the foundation that the New Testament was written in the first century AD by many of the Apostles while alive is a scam perpetrated by the West and Western civilization.
32. Finally, if the story of Jesus were indeed true, we should have expected that Jews in Israel and around the globe would have been mostly Christians by the time Jesus died and thereafter.
33. But today, there are hardly any Christians of Jewish origin in Israel.
34. And Christians are everywhere else other than in Israel.
35. The New Testament contains absolutely nothing that can be perceived as true and factual other than profound words and a very enticing, alluring, and seducing storyline.
36. The most deceptive idea is that we can commit sin and easily inherit heaven on earth and the afterlife by simply being Jesus-believers.
37. The British concocted a new story, demoting Mother Mary and promoting Jesus to start a new church called the Anglican Church and a new treasury at Canterbury.
38. It is all about stealing money by coveting and stealing land, as ordained by the self-created God.
39. **THE BRITISH DO HAVE TALENT INDEED.**
40. **Finally, we conclude that the British invented the story of Jesus only to cheat and gain.**

References:


a) Christian Population in Israel: https://www.timesofisrael.com/annual-christmas-report-says-israels-christian-population-has-grown-to-185000/
b) Population of Israel: **https://www.timesofisrael.com/israels-population-approaches-9-7-million-as-2022-comes-to-an-end/**
c) Latest Population Statistics for Israel: **https://www.timesofisrael.com/israels-population-approaches-9-7-million-as-2022-comes-to-an-end/**
d) Videos, debates, and presentations by Rabbi Michel Skobac in Jews for Judaism; **https://jewsforjudaism.org/staff**
e) Western propaganda on the Bible by highly reputable Jesus-deniers.
f) Those are extensive and argue that the New Testament contains too many anomalies, but there is no fraud or conspiracy in its publication.
g) Those include books, YouTube videos, podcasts, debates etc. on the truth of the story of Jesus:
    i)     By Dr. Bart D. Ehrman: **https://en.wikipedia.org/wiki/Bart_D._Ehrman**
    ii)     By Dr. David Skrbina: **https://www.davidskrbina.com/**
    iii)     By Derek Lambert of MythVision podcasts: **https://www.youtube.com/@MythVisionPodcast**

h) Did Jesus exist: Yes: by Open Mind: **https://www.bbvaopenmind.com/en/science/scientific-insights/did-jesus-of-nazareth-actually-exist-the-evidence-says-yes/**


***

Volume 7

# SLIPS, COVER-UP LIES, SPINS AND ANOMALIES OF JESUS

## Volume 7- Slips, Cover-up Lies, Spins and Anomalies of Jesus

This Volume 7 is a copy of Volume 3, published in the book "**British Invented Jesus to Cheat and Win."**

(volume numbers and chapter numbers are amended here to avoid confusion)

# Volume 7- Slips, Cover-up Lies, Spins and Anomalies of Jesus

## Volume 7: Ch: 1- Dead Men Walking in Streets of Jerusalem (SPIN)

### HIGHLIGHTS

* Gospel of Matthew, with so many lies and spins, proved the truth *
*** Clearly, the story of Jesus is an invention ***
******************************************

1. The Gospel of Matthew presents many Spins (baffling stories that create wonderment) from the beginning to the end.

2. The Gospel of Mathew started with these Spins:

    a) God appeared to Mary and informed her about her virgin pregnancy.
    b) Three wise men from the East chased a star to Bethlehem.
    c) Herod the Great ordered an Infanticide around Bethlehem.
    d) Joseph, Mary, and Jesus fled to Egypt to escape the Infanticide as directed by God.

3. These spins disappeared from all other Gospels, apparently realizing the stupidity of the stories.

4. Moreover, the Gospel of Luke denied God's direction to Joseph. It claimed that they could not have gone to Egypt since they departed from Jerusalem and went home to Galilee when Jesus was eight (8) days old, soon after his circumcision.

5. But nothing is more incredible & ludicrous in the Gospel of Matthew than the colossal earthquake when Jesus died on the cross and the subsequent events due to the earthquake.

6. The earthquake also disappeared from all other Gospels, proving that these are not true testimonies but fake stories.

7. The Gospel of Mathew stated the following Spins:

    a) There was a huge earthquake around the world (not just in Jerusalem or in Israel but the earth shook) at the very second Jesus breathed his last.
    b) The curtain at the temple was torn into two from top to bottom.
    c) The rocks split and tombs broke open with many dead people coming out of their tombs and walking in the streets.

8. We read the following in chapter 27 of the Gospel of Matthew:

    *Mt. 27:50   And when Jesus had cried out again in a loud voice, he gave up his spirit.*

*Mt. 27:51*   At that moment the curtain of the temple was torn in two from top to bottom. The earth shook and the rocks split.

*Mt. 27:52*   **The tombs broke open and the bodies of many holy people who had died were raised to life.**

*Mt. 27:53*   **They came out of the tombs, and after Jesus' resurrection they went into the holy city and appeared to many people.**

*Mt. 27:54*   When the centurion and those with him who were guarding Jesus saw the earthquake and all that had happened, they were terrified, and exclaimed, "Surely he was the Son [Or a son] of God!"

9. By reading the Gospel further, we can deduce that there was no earthquake, not even at Golgotha, where two robbers and Jesus were crucified.

10. We can conclude the same since none of the other three Gospel writers mentions this incredible event.

11. Rocks split, but the three crosses did not break & fall.

12. Centurion (Roman Commander) and Roman soldiers remained guarding the crucifixion as though nothing had happened.

13. The women who are there specially to act as witnesses to the crucifixion remained there cooly without panic.

14. The Gospel did not state whether the dead men walking went home or entered their tombs with no complaint!

15. **The Gospel of Matthew proved the truth: the story of Jesus is a scam.**

***

# Volume 7- Slips, Cover-up Lies, Spins and Anomalies of Jesus

## Volume 7: Ch: 2- Apostle Paul and Spain (Slip)

### HIGHLIGHTS
* By using the word "Spain" in the epistle to the Romans, the fraud was revealed *
* The word "SPAIN" did not exist until 1492 AD *
* West jointly invented the story of Jesus after 1492 AD *
*** Clearly, the story of Jesus is an invention ***
*******************************************

16.  Apostle Paul destroyed the entire New Testament by using the word "**Spain**" two times in the epistle to the Romans *(V2B Ch 8)*.

17.  Romans 15: 24 read as follows:

*"I plan to do so when I go to **Spain**. I hope to visit you while passing through and to have you assist me on my journey there, after I have enjoyed your company for a while".*

18.  Romans 15: 28 read as follows:

*"So after I have completed this task and have made sure that they have received this fruit, I will go to **Spain** and visit you on the way".*

19.  The word "**Spain**" or the country "**Spain**" did not exist until 1492, when Spain was formed.

20.  During the first two centuries AD, when Romans ruled, this whole peninsula (now known as Spain and Portugal) was known only as Hispania or the Iberian Peninsula.

21.  In the first century AD, this region was unknown under the Roman Empire as it held no significance to the larger world.

22.  It is important to note that throughout the New Testament, the Mastermind used names of countries that existed in the first century AD, except in cases like this when he slipped.

23.  The story of Jesus is written after 1492, faking that it was written in the first century AD.

24.  Clearly, the Mastermind had some incentive for that misleading scheme.

25.  The British Mastermind was incentivized to disconnect the writing of the Gospels demoting Mother Mary and promoting Jesus and the consequent creation of the Anglican Church demoting Mother Mary and promoting Jesus.

26.  **The deception is dead clear, inventing a God to cheat and win.**

References:

a) History of Spain: La Moncloa:

**https://www.lamoncloa.gob.es/lang/en/espana/historyandculture/history/Paginas/index.aspx#:~:text=By%201492%20the%20united%20Spain,pot%20of%20the%20three%20cultures**

b) Hispania: Wikipedia: **https://en.wikipedia.org/wiki/Hispania**

c) Spain: Wikipedia: **https://en.wikipedia.org/wiki/Spain**

***

# Volume 7- Slips, Cover-up Lies, Spins and Anomalies of Jesus

### Volume 7: Ch: 3- Apostle John and Paper (A Slip)

## HIGHLIGHTS

* By using the word "**paper**" in the epistle of 2 John, the fraud was again revealed *
* The word "**paper**" did not exist until 200 AD *
* West jointly invented the story of Jesus and faked it as written in the first century AD *
*** Clearly, the story of Jesus is an invention of the West ***
***************************************

27. The story of Jesus and the New Testament is substantially founded on two presumptions:

   a) The twenty-seven (27) books, including the four (4) Gospels, were written by then-living Apostles.
   b) All are written in the first century AD.

28. Both are non-negotiable foundations since Apostle Paul is writing: "I, Paul, write this greeting in my own hand" (1 Corinthians 16:21); "See what large letters I write to you with my own hands" (Galatians 6:11); "I, Paul, write this greeting in my own hand" (Colossians 4:18); "I, Paul, write this greeting in my own hand which is the distinguishing mark in all my letters; this is how I write" (2 Thessalonians 3:17); "I, Paul, am writing this with my own hand" (Philemon 19).

29. Apostle Paul appears to be so desperate to emphasize to people well known to him that he was writing the letters and not some imposters writing it. This is very odd.

30. In addition, Apostle Paul is also desperate to let them know that he was not lying, which he repeats three places (Romans 9:1; 2 Corinthians 11;31; 1 Timothy 2:7).

31. This is too unusual and suspicious.

32. In the last chapter, we have seen beyond any doubt that the Epistle to Romans, assumed to be written by Apostle Paul, was written after 1492 and, therefore, not written by him due to the usage of the word "Spain."

33. Both foundations of the New Testament fell off by the slip of the imposters, acting as a living Apostle Paul.

34. Apostle John also destroyed the entire New Testament by using the word "paper" once in the epistle known as 2 John, written by him (2 John 12).

35. We have established positively that the character depicted as Apostle John, "the disciple whom Jesus loved" & the highly glorified as a monumental prophet by the current Jesus-

believers of the West, was highly suspicious and that the character depicted as Apostle John was an imposter, faking that a living Apostle John wrote the Gospel of John.

36. Epistle 2 John, depicted as written by Apostle John, drove the last nail on the coffins of not only Apostle John but also in the New Testament.

37. This Epistle is depicted as a second letter written by Apostle John.

38. There is nothing in the letter to suggest who wrote it. Someone named it 2 John, and the name only leads us to assume that the Apostle John wrote it.

39. The epistles are full of names, mostly Jews with Greek names. But this letter is written to "dear lady" without naming her.

40. 2 John 12 read as follows:

> "I have much to write to you, but I do not want to use **paper** and ink. Instead, I hope to visit you and talk with you face to face, so that our joy may be complete".

41. How can we claim that the above verse destroyed both the foundations of the Story of Jesus and the New Testament?

42. The word "**paper**" or any "**paper**" never existed in the first century AD.

43. The paper was invented by the Chinese in 200 AD., But this never reached the West before 1200 AD.

44. Only after 1200 AD, this word existed in the West, the true origin of the Bible.

45. Now we have "**paper**," the slip of Apostle John, to supplement the slip of Apostle Paul by using the word "Spain."

46. If Apostle Paul and Apostle John are imposters, Jesus must be a fake character.

47. We have established that Jesus and all the Jewish characters in the Gospels were not Jews but Greeks *(V1 Ch 17)*.

48. **The deception of the West is dead clear, inventing a God to cheat and win.**


References:


d) History of paper by American Forest & Paper Association: **https://www.afandpa.org/news/2021/history-paper#:~:text=About%202%2C000%20years%20ago%2C%20inventors,Lun%2C%20a%20Chinese%20court%20official**.

e) Papermaking Process by Brittanica: **https://www.britannica.com/technology/papermaking**

f) Papermaking by Wikipedia: **https://en.wikipedia.org/wiki/Papermaking#:~:text=Papermaking%2C%20regardless%20of%20the%20scale,of%20fibres%20using%20a%20press**.

g) When was 2 John written? **https://www.churchofjesuschrist.org/study/manual/new-testament-seminary-teacher-manual/introduction-to-the-second-epistle-of-john?lang=eng**

h) Second John- Pastor Chuck Swindol: **https://insight.org/resources/bible/the-general-epistles/second-john**

i) Second Epistle of John: Wikipedia: **https://en.wikipedia.org/wiki/Second_Epistle_of_John**

j) Second Epistle of John: New World Encyclopedia: **https://www.newworldencyclopedia.org/entry/Second_Epistle_of_John**

k)   An Introduction to book of 2 John: **https://bible.org/article/introduction-book-2-john**

l)   Videos, debates, and presentations by Rabbi Michel Skobac in Jews for Judaism; **https://jewsforjudaism.org/staff**

m)   Western propaganda on the Bible by highly reputable Jesus-deniers.

n)   Those are extensive & argue that there are too many anomalies in the New Testament, but there is no fraud or conspiracy in the publication of the New Testament.

o)   Those include books, YouTube videos, podcasts, debates etc. on the truth of the story of Jesus:

    i)       By Dr. Bart D. Ehrman: **https://en.wikipedia.org/wiki/Bart_D._Ehrman**

    ii)      By Dr.  David Skrbina:  **https://www.davidskrbina.com/**

    iii)    By Derek Lambert of MythVision podcasts: **https://www.youtube.com/@MythVisionPodcast**

p)   Did Jesus exist: Yes: by Open Mind: **https://www.bbvaopenmind.com/en/science/scientific-insights/did-jesus-of-nazareth-actually-exist-the-evidence-says-yes/**

***

## Volume 7- Slips, Cover-up Lies, Spins and Anomalies of Jesus

## Volume 7: Ch: 4- Jews are Greeks (A Slip & A Cover-Up Lie)

### HIGHLIGHTS
* Jesus claimed that applying spices on bodies for burial was good *
* The Gospel of John claimed that applying spices was according to Jewish burial customs *
* It was a lie to cover up the slip in the three synoptic Gospels *
* Jesus and the disciples were not Jews *
These characters were Greeks acting as Jews *
*** Clearly, the story of Jesus is an invention of the West to cheat and win ***
******************************************

49.  In every Gospel, there is a story of some lady, mostly all alone among Jesus and his entourage, pouring spice on Jesus and massaging Jesus while the men remain watching and complaining that the lady is wasting money that could have been used for the poor.

50.  But Jesus reprimands them and praises the lady for "preparing Jesus for his burial."

51.  All are supposed to be Jews, and they did not say that using spice was not appropriate for preparing the body for burial.

52.  All three synoptic Gospels have this story, but the lady is not identified by name.

53.  However, the Gospel of John tells this story differently. Here, the lady is Mary, sister of Lazarus, whom Jesus resurrected a few days earlier.

54.  She did the spice "pouring and massaging" during a massive party of Jews, all celebrating the miracle of the raising of Lazarus from the dead by Jesus.

55.  The fact that Jesus and all the Jews accepted the spice story could not be retracted as three synoptic Gospels had established that using spices in bodies for burial was a Jewish custom.

56.  By now, the Mastermind has realized that applying spices to bodies for burial is strictly prohibited by Jewish laws.

57.   So, the only option for the writers of the Gospel of John was to cover up the intractable slip and reinforce the slip.

58.  Gospel of John, who invented the story of raising Lazarus from the dead, invented a story that Nicodemus suddenly appeared in Jerusalem from nowhere with seventy- five pounds of spices, joined Joseph of Arimathea, and applied all that spice to bury Jesus by leaving is a very large cave.

59.  In all three synoptic Gospels, there was no mention of Nicodemus at all.

60. The Gospel of John sealed the slip by another lie.

61. The Gospel of John states the lie in John 19:40:

    *"Taking Jesus' body, the two of them wrapped it, with the spices, in strips of linen. **This was in accordance with Jewish burial customs**".*

62. On the other hand, it is a normal custom for Greeks to pour perfume from an alabaster jar onto bodies for burial.

63. **We can conclude that the character Jesus, all the disciples, and Mary Magdalene, who made an extraordinary effort to get spices to apply to Jesus' body on Easter Sunday, were not Jews but Greeks.**

64. It is important to note that all twenty-seven books of the New Testament were originally written in Greek, as per the West.

65. It is quite clear that the West, who invented this story, could not find Jews to write this story of Jesus in Hebrew language or Aramaic language.

66. We can conclude that the characters of Jesus, all the disciples, including Apostle John and Mary Magdalene, who made an extraordinary effort to get spices to apply to Jesus' body on Easter Sunday, were not Jews but Greeks.

67. **We can further conclude that the story of Jesus in the New Testament was invented to cheat and win.**


References:


q) Embalming (preserve body from decaying by applying spices) of body for burial is prohibited by Jewish Law: Rabbi Michael Pont: **https://images.shulcloud.com/1220/uploads/MJCdeathmourningbooklet.pdf**

r) Burial customs of Jews: Rohatyn Jewish Heritage & **https://rohatynjewishheritage.org/en/culture/death-burial-mourning/**

s) Burial customs of Jews: **www.shiva.com** & **https://www.shiva.com/learning-center/death-and-mourning/jewish-funerals-and-burial**

t) Burial Customs of Greeks: **https://en.m.wikipedia.org/wiki/Ancient_Greek_funeral_and_burial_practices#**

u) Apostle John died at the age of 93 around AD 100: Wikipedia: **https://en.wikipedia.org/wiki/John_the_Apostle**

v) Apostle John write the Gospel of John and John was buried at Ephesus in Greece: **https://en.wikipedia.org/wiki/John_the_Apostle**

w) Apostle John died in AD 101: New World Encyclopedia: **https://www.newworldencyclopedia.org/entry/John_the_Apostle**

x) Apostle John died in AD 100: Catholics online: **https://www.catholic.org/saints/saint.php?saint_id=228**

y) Gospel of John is fraud: American Atheists: **https://www.atheists.org/activism/resources/did-jesus-exist/**



*** 

# Volume 7- Slips, Cover-up Lies, Spins and Anomalies of Jesus

## Volume 7: Ch: 5- Jerusalem, Mount of Olives and Bethany (A Slip & A Cover-Up Lie)

### HIGHLIGHTS

* The Apostles utter many lies to cover up the false story of Jesus *
* The Gospel of John falsely claims that Bethany was only 3 km from Jerusalem, knowing that it was 12 km in truth *
* The Gospel of John falsely claims that Jesus and his disciples did not walk up to the Mount of Olives after the Last Supper *
* The Book of Acts falsely claims that Mount of Olives was only 1.1 km from Jerusalem, knowing that it was 5 km in truth *
* There were all lies to cover up the slip in the three synoptic Gospels *
* The story writers, the Apostles, were never in Jerusalem *
*** Clearly, the story of Jesus is an invention of the West to cheat and win ***
*****************************************

68. In the New Testament, only two distances between places are mentioned, though hundreds of places are named.

69. Both are Cover-Up lies.

70. Both are lies to cover up serious impossibilities written in the stories in all three Synoptic Gospels, which could not be edited, corrected, or retracted.

71. The stories were written by people who have never been to these places, which again proves that "**Jews are Greeks**".

72. You can come to these conclusions only if you analyze facts of the stories written with the true related facts: in this case, geography around these three places.

73. The true distance between Jerusalem and the Mount of Olives is about 5 kilometers, but the terrain makes the travel very cumbersome, particularly at night.

74. But the Book of Acts claims without any reason that the distance between Jerusalem and the Mount of Olives was just 1.1 km (Acts 1: 12).

75. Acts 1: 12 read:

    *"Then they returned to Jerusalem from the hill called the Mount of Olives, a Sabbath day's walk [That is, about 3/4 of a mile (about 1,100 meters)] from the city".*

76. The distance written was a **mammoth lie**: 1.1 km instead of 5 kilometers: a lie to lessen the impossibility of the relevant story *(V2B Ch 3; V2C 3)*.

77. Similarly, the true distance between Jerusalem & Bethany is about 12 kilometers, but the terrain makes the travel very cumbersome, particularly at night.

78. But without any reason, the Gospel of John claims that the distance between Jerusalem and Bethany was less than 3 km (John 11: 18).

79. John 11: 18 read:

    *"Bethany was less than two miles [Greek: fifteen stadia (about 3 kilometres)] from Jerusalem,"*

80. The distance written was another **mammoth lie**: 3 km instead of 12 kilometers: a lie to lessen the impossibility of the relevant story *(V2B Ch 3; V2C 3)*.

81. If the true distances and the time taken to walk these distances are understood and analyzed with the stories from the Hosanna Sunday to Good Friday, each story collapses *( V2C 1-9)*.

82. The stories and timings are sealed and stamped in the synoptic Gospels and cannot be amended, edited, or retracted.

83. The only option was to lie and hope that nobody would analyze these serious anomalies in the word of God.

84. There was another serious lie related to these lies in the Gospel of John.

85. The three synoptic Gospels all claimed that Jesus and his disciples walked to the Mount of Olives after the Last Supper.

86. There, they prayed, and Jesus foretold Peter's three denials (Matthew 26: 30-35; Mark 14: 26-31; Luke 22: 39-40).

87. Again, the story that they walked to the Mount of Olives after the Last Supper could not be amended, edited, or retracted.

88. And we can see the "cover-up lie"; according to the Gospel of John, Jesus and his disciples did not walk to the Mount of Olives but walked straight to an "olive grove" in the Kidron Valley after the Last Supper; trying to make the story less impossible (John 18: 1).

89. The Gospel of John provided two escape routes for the fake stories: first, the distance was only 1.1 kilometers, and second, they did not climb Mount Olives in any case.

90. We can conclude that the three synoptic Gospels were written by people who have never been to Jerusalem and the surrounding areas.

91. Surely, they never climbed up and down Jerusalem, Mount of Olives, or Bethany.

92. **We can conclude that imposters, most possibly British, under a mastermind, are inventing the story of Jesus to cheat and win.**

References:

    z)   Jerusalem and Jerico: **https://talmidimway.org/post/next-gospel-backgrounds-lesson-triumphal-entry-part-i/**

    aa) Bethany on Wikipedia: **https://en.wikipedia.org/wiki/Bethany**

    bb) Kidron Valley-YouTube: **https://www.youtube.com/watch?v=0JEkM0imfok**

    cc) Last days of Jesus Timeline: **https://www.biblestudy.org/maps/last-days-of-jesus-timeline.html**

dd) Videos, debates, and presentations by Rabbi Michel Skobac in Jews for Judaism;
**https://jewsforjudaism.org/staff**
ee) Western propaganda on the Bible by highly reputable Jesus-deniers.
ff) Those are extensive and argue that the New Testament contains too many anomalies; yet they conclude that there was no fraud or conspiracy in its publication.
gg) Those include books, YouTube videos, podcasts, debates etc. on the truth of the story of Jesus:
    iv) By Dr. Bart D. Ehrman: **https://en.wikipedia.org/wiki/Bart_D._Ehrman**
    v) By Dr. David Skrbina: **https://www.davidskrbina.com/**
    vi) By Derek Lambert of MythVision podcasts: **https://www.youtube.com/@MythVisionPodcast**
hh) Did Jesus exist: Yes: by Open Mind: **https://www.bbvaopenmind.com/en/science/scientific-insights/did-jesus-of-nazareth-actually-exist-the-evidence-says-yes/**

***

# Volume 7- Slips, Cover-up Lies, Spins and Anomalies of Jesus

## Volume 7: Ch: 6- Paul Did not Meet All the Disciples (A Slip & A Lie)

### HIGHLIGHTS

* The Apostle Paul says in Galatians that he did not meet Apostle Peter for three years after his vision *
* And he did not meet any other disciples other than Peter and James *
* But the Book of Acts claimed that Apostle Paul went straight to Jerusalem and stayed with all the disciples *
* Greek story writers are writing complex fictional stories with no coordination *
*** Clearly, the story of Jesus is an invention of the West to cheat and win ***
***************************************

93. We have seen that Apostle Paul is a hijacker of the original scheme of Jesus who appointed Apostle Peter as the rock of the church *(V2D Ch 1)*.

94. Instead, Apostle Paul became the rock of the Church.

95. We can see from his claims that Apostle Paul was a boastful hijacker.

96. He insisted that the disciples did not teach him or prepare him for the ministry; he learned everything directly from God.

97. Apostle Paul wrote many epistles by his own hand.

98. He wrote in the Epistle to Galatians @Ch 6: 11:

> *"See what large letters I use as I write to you with my own hand!"*

99. This clearly meant that Apostle Paul wrote this Epistle.

100. Then, he boldly and incredibly wrote that after his vision on a road in Damascus, Syria, he never went to Jerusalem and never met any disciple, including Apostle Peter, for three years.

101. Apostle Paul claims that he met only Apostle Paul and James (the brother of Jesus) and that he did not meet the other disciples.

102. In the first chapter of Galatians, Apostle Paul wrote:

| | |
|---|---|
| *Ga. 1:13* | *For you have heard of my previous way of life in Judaism, how intensely I persecuted the church of God and tried to destroy it.* |
| *Ga. 1:14* | *I was advancing in Judaism beyond many Jews of my own age and was extremely zealous for the traditions of my fathers.* |
| *Ga. 1:15* | *But when God, who set me apart from birth [Or from my mother's womb] and called me by his grace, was pleased* |
| *Ga. 1:16* | *to reveal his Son in me so that I might preach him among the Gentiles, I did not consult any man,* |

| | |
|---|---|
| *Ga. 1:17* | *nor did I go up to Jerusalem to see those who were apostles before I was, but I went immediately into Arabia and later returned to Damascus.* |
| *Ga. 1:18* | ***Then after three years, I went up to Jerusalem to get acquainted with Peter [Greek: Cephas] and stayed with him fifteen days.*** |
| *Ga. 1:19* | ***I saw none of the other apostles — only James, the Lord's brother.*** |
| *Ga. 1:20* | *I assure you before God that what I am writing to you is no lie.* |
| *Ga. 1:21* | *Later I went to Syria and Cilicia.* |
| *Ga. 1:22* | *I was personally unknown to the churches of Judea that are in Christ.* |
| *Ga. 1:23* | *They only heard the report: "The man who formerly persecuted us is now preaching the faith he once tried to destroy."* |
| *Ga. 1:24* | *And they praised God because of me.* |

103. But the Book of Acts, presumably written by Luke, Paul's disciple, there is a very contradictory version of the events; that Apostle Paul, after his vision, went straight to Jerusalem, saw all the disciples, preached in Jerusalem before starting his mission as "ambassador of the gentiles."

104. This meant that Apostle Paul went and saw all the disciples and stayed with them in Jerusalem soon after his vision and before he started his ministry overseas, mainly in Greece.

105. The Book of Acts, Chapter 9, read as follows:

| | |
|---|---|
| *Ac. 9:23* | *After many days had gone by, the Jews conspired to kill him,* |
| *Ac. 9:24* | *but Saul learned of their plan. Day and night they kept close watch on the city gates in order to kill him.* |
| *Ac. 9:25* | *But his followers took him by night and lowered him in a basket through an opening in the wall.* |
| *Ac. 9:26* | *When he came to Jerusalem, he tried to join the disciples, but they were all afraid of him, not believing that he really was a disciple.* |
| *Ac. 9:27* | *But Barnabas took him and brought him to the apostles. He told them how Saul on his journey had seen the Lord and that the Lord had spoken to him, and how in Damascus he had preached fearlessly in the name of Jesus.* |
| *Ac. 9:28* | ***So Saul stayed with them and moved about freely in Jerusalem, speaking boldly in the name of the Lord.*** |
| *Ac. 9:29* | *He talked and debated with the Grecian Jews, but they tried to kill him.* |
| *Ac. 9:30* | *When the brothers learned of this, they took him down to Caesarea and sent him off to Tarsus.* |

106. We can conclude that the Mastermind, after publishing the Book of Acts, changed the storyline to convey that Apostle Paul did not learn anything from Apostle Peter or any disciples but from God directly.

107. But the real conclusion is that a mastermind with many Greek story writers, without any good knowledge of Israel, Jerusalem, or Jewish customs, was impersonating Apostles and writing very complex and complicated fictional stories of the first century AD with no coordination between them; they invented stories likely in the sixteenth century AD.

References:

ii) Preparation of Paul: **https://www.ligonier.org/learn/devotionals/the-preparation-of-paul**

jj) Thangs Paul and Luke: **https://thingspaulandluke.wordpress.com/2015/12/26/pauls-official-meeting-with-the-apostles/**

kk) Why did Paul go to Arabia: **https://readingacts.com/2017/09/08/why-did-paul-go-to-arabia/**

ll) After conversion, did Paul immediately begin his ministry or go to Arabia : **https://adornthegospel.com/2020/07/14/after-conversion-did-paul-immediately-begin-his-ministry-or-go-to-arabia/**

mm) Videos, debates, and presentations by Rabbi Michel Skobac in Jews for Judaism; **https://jewsforjudaism.org/staff**

nn) Western propaganda on the Bible by highly reputable Jesus-deniers.

oo) Those are extensive and argue that the New Testament contains too many anomalies, yet they conclude that there was no fraud or conspiracy in its publication.

pp) Those include books, YouTube videos, podcasts, debates etc. on the truth of the story of Jesus:

    vii) By Dr. Bart D. Ehrman: **https://en.wikipedia.org/wiki/Bart_D._Ehrman**

    viii) By Dr. David Skrbina: **https://www.davidskrbina.com/**

    ix) By Derek Lambert of MythVision podcasts: **https://www.youtube.com/@MythVisionPodcast**

qq) Did Jesus exist: Yes: by Open Mind: **https://www.bbvaopenmind.com/en/science/scientific-insights/did-jesus-of-nazareth-actually-exist-the-evidence-says-yes/**

***

Volume 8

# SELLING ETERNAL LIFE BY FRAUD

## Volume 8- Selling Eternal Life by Forgery.

This Volume 8 is a copy of Volume 6, published in the book **"British Invented Jesus to Cheat and Win."**

(volume numbers and chapter numbers are amended here to avoid confusion)

# Volume 8 (6)- Selling Eternal Life by Forgery

# Unschooled and uneducated Apostles wrote the Gospels and Epistles

All the presumed writers of the gospels and epistles were the disciples of Jesus, and they were all illiterate and unschooled. This meant that they could not even read, never mind write. And writing on Scrolls in the first century AD was a very special skill that only a few people possessed. This meant that we should not expect Apostle John, Apostle Peter, and even Apostle Paul to be able to write anything at all. Not only did they claim that they wrote, but they also claimed that they were writing in their own hands. Such an emphasis is unwarranted unless trying to negate the truth.

### (From the Book of Acts)

**Ac. 4:13**     When they saw the courage of Peter and John and realized that they were unschooled, ordinary men, they were astonished, and they took note that these men had been with Jesus.

**Ac. 4:14**     But since they could see the man who had been healed standing there with them, there was nothing they could say.

### (From the book of Galatians and of Philemon)

**Ga. 1:20**     I assure you before God that what I am writing to you is no lie.

**Phile. 19**     I, Paul, am writing this with my own hand. I will pay it back
— not to mention that you owe me your very self.

### (From the book of 1 John)

**1Jn. 2:7**     Dear friends, I am not writing you a new command but an old one, which you have had since the beginning. This old command is the message you have heard.

**1Jn. 2:8**     Yet I am writing you a new command; its truth is seen in him and you, because the darkness is passing and the true light is already shining.

### (From the book of 2 Thessalonians)

**2Th. 3:17**     I, Paul, write this greeting in my own hand, which is the distinguishing mark in all my letters. This is how I write.

+++

# Bethlehem and Virgin Birth

The New Testament stands on the proposition that Jesus was prophesized to be born in Bethlehem, the city of King David. That was based on a prophecy. You can see that Apostle Matthew changed Bethlehem Ephrathah, a king and a person, into a place to fit his storyline. The word "Ephrathah" was removed so that a person became a place. This is just one example of the extensive forgery in the New Testament to sell the eternal life of Jesus.

### (From the Gospel of Matthew)

Mt. 2:2     and asked, "Where is the one who has been born king of the Jews? We saw his star in the east [Or star when it rose] and have come to worship him."

Mt. 2:3     When King Herod heard this he was disturbed, and all Jerusalem with him.

Mt. 2:4     When he had called together all the people's chief priests and teachers of the law, he asked them where the Christ [Or Messiah] was to be born.

Mt. 2:5     "In Bethlehem in Judea," they replied, "for this is what the prophet has written:

Mt. 2:6     "'But you, Bethlehem, in the land of Judah, are by no means least among the rulers of Judah; for out of you will come a ruler who will be the shepherd of my people Israel.'" [Micah 5:2]

+++

### (From the Book of Micah)

Mi. 5:1     Marshal your troops, O city of troops, [Or Strengthen your walls, O walled city] for a siege is laid against us. They will strike Israel's ruler on the cheek with a rod.

Mi. 5:2     "But you, Bethlehem Ephrathah, though you are small among the clans [Or rulers] of Judah, out of you will come for me one who will be ruler over Israel, whose origins [Hebrew goings out] are from of old, from ancient times." [Or from days of eternity]

+++

### (From the book of 1 Chronicles)

1Ch. 2:50     These were the descendants of Caleb. The sons of Hur the firstborn of Ephrathah: Shobal the father of Kiriath Jearim,

1Ch. 2:51     Salma the father of Bethlehem, and Hareph the father of Beth Gader.

+++

# My Testimony or His Testimony or Our Testimony

After completing his Gospel with Chapter 20, Apostle John, later, after years, added Chapter 21 to create an impression that he was writing it personally while he was alive. That attempt proved the opposite. The newly added chapter ended with two verses: "His testimony," "My testimony," and "We know," mixing up and proving the truth. These proved conclusively that the Gospel writer was impersonating a living Apostle John.

If the Apostle John was an impersonator, then we should assume that all the originators of the 27 books, including the four Gospels, are impersonators.


**(From the Gospel of John)**

**Jn. 21:24**    **This is the disciple who testifies to these things and who wrote them down. We know that his testimony is true.**

**Jn. 21:25**    **Jesus did many other things as well. If every one of them were written down, I suppose that even the whole world would not have room for the books that would be written.**


**+++**

**Who are "we" in this verse 24?**

**Obviously, the mastermind and his team.**

**+++**

**Who is "I" in this verse 25?**

**Obviously, the mastermind and his team.**

**+++**

**Whose testimony is in "his testimony" in this verse 24?**

**Obviously, of the mastermind and his team.**

**+++**

# Spices in Jewish Burials: Is Jesus a Jew or Greek?

Embalming of bodies for burial is strictly prohibited by Jewish Laws for burial as bodies must be returned to earth with no delay.

We conclude that all the Jewish characters, including Jesus, were not indeed Jews but Greeks.

### (From the Gospel of John)

**Jn. 19:39**   He was accompanied by Nicodemus, the man who earlier had visited Jesus at night. Nicodemus brought a mixture of myrrh and aloes, about seventy-five pounds. [Greek: a hundred litrai (about 34 kilograms)]

**Jn. 19:40**   Taking Jesus' body, the two of them wrapped it, with the spices, in strips of linen. This was in accordance with Jewish burial customs.

**Jn. 19:41**   At the place where Jesus was crucified, there was a garden, and in the garden a new tomb, in which no-one had ever been laid.

**Jn. 19:42**   Because it was the Jewish day of Preparation and since the tomb was near by, they laid Jesus there.

+++

**Jn. 12:3**   Then Mary took about a pint [Greek: a litra (probably about 0.5 litre)] of pure nard, an expensive perfume; she poured it on Jesus' feet and wiped his feet with her hair. And the house was filled with the fragrance of the perfume.

**Jn. 12:4**   But one of his disciples, Judas Iscariot, who was later to betray him, objected,

**Jn. 12:5**   "Why wasn't this perfume sold and the money given to the poor? It was worth a year's wages." [Greek: three hundred denarii]

**Jn. 12:6**   He did not say this because he cared about the poor but because he was a thief; as keeper of the money bag, he used to help himself to what was put into it.

**Jn. 12:7**   "Leave her alone," Jesus replied. "It was intended that she should save this perfume for the day of my burial.

**Jn. 12:8**   You will always have the poor among you, but you will not always have me."

+++

**Lk. 24:1**   On the first day of the week, very early in the morning, the women took the spices they had prepared and went to the tomb.

**Lk. 24:2**   They found the stone rolled away from the tomb,

+++

## Paul's Desperation to visit Spain

The word Spain" of the country known today as "Spain" did not exist until 1498. Before that, Spain and Portugal were two regions known as Iberia or the Iberian Peninsula. Nobody in Israel or Judea knew much about that region in the first century AD. In other words, nobody could have used the word "Spain" unless much after 1498 when the name Spain became known to far way regions like the region surrounding Judea or today's Israel.

But the Mastermind, impersonating Jews, Apostles, and Saints living in the first century AD, slipped and wrote the word "Spain" twice in the Book of Romans in chapter 15, which is assumed to have been written by Apostle Paul before 100 AD.

Ro. 15:24    I plan to do so when I go to **Spain**. I hope to visit you while passing through and to have you assist me on my journey there, after I have enjoyed your company for a while.

Ro. 15:25    Now, however, I am on my way to Jerusalem in the service of the saints there.

Ro. 15:26    For Macedonia and Achaia were pleased to make a contribution for the poor among the saints in Jerusalem.

Ro. 15:27    They were pleased to do it, and indeed they owe it to them.
For if the Gentiles have shared in the Jews' spiritual blessings, they owe it to the Jews to share with them their material blessings.

Ro. 15:28    So after I have completed this task and have made sure that they have received this fruit, I will go to **Spain** and visit you on the way.

## This reinforced the fraud of the story of Jesus and of the New Testament.

+++

# Paper and Ink

The word "paper" did not exist in the Middle East and Europe until 1200AD-1400 AD. This proved beyond any doubt that Apostle John, who lived in the first century, did not write the epistle and that the New Testament was originally written later than 1200 AD.

*"I have much to write to you, but I do not want to use paper and ink. Instead, I hope to visit you and talk with you face to face, so that our joy may be complete".*
(2 John 12)

It was supposedly written by Apostle John in 95 AD. It is from the city of Ephesus, while paper was first invented in China in 200 AD. Paper was known in the Middle East only by 800 AD and in Europe by 1200 AD.

## This was the final nail in the coffin of the New Testament.

Imagine Mahatma Gandhi, who died in 1948, writing, "I always talked to Pandit Nehru on my mobile phone!"
+++

Volume 9

# ILLUSTRATIONS & MAPS

## <u>Volume 9- Illustrations and Maps</u>

This Volume 9 is a copy of Volume 7, published in the book **"British Invented Jesus to Cheat and Win."**

(volume numbers and chapter numbers are amended here to avoid confusion)

## Views of Jerusalem & Mount of Olives from Kidron Valley

Jerusalem is made inaccessible to protect it from invasions, making it a laborious walk of more than two kilometers each way to climb up and down from the Kidron Valley to Jerusalem.
(V2B. Ch 2)

+++

# Jesus' Dilemma: Jews are Greeks, Babylon is Rome, Paul is Peter

## Mount of Olives

The Mount of Olives, 3500 feet above the Kidron Valley, is 5 kilometers from Jerusalem. Then, suddenly, the Book of Acts says without any apparent reason that Mount Olives is only 1.1 kilometers from Jerusalem.
(V2B Ch 2; V2B Ch 17; V2B Ch 18; etc.)
+++

# Jesus' Dilemma: Jews are Greeks, Babylon is Rome, Paul is Peter

## <u>Bethany</u>

Bethany is 12 kilometers from Jerusalem, but suddenly, the Gospel of John says, without any apparent reason or context, that Bethany is only 3 kilometers from Jerusalem.
(V2B Ch 2; V2B Ch 17; V2B Ch 18; etc.)

+++

# Jesus' Dilemma: Jews are Greeks, Babylon is Rome, Paul is Peter

## The Hosanna, the Triumphant Entry to Jerusalem

## Cursing of the fig tree on the way from Bethany to Jerusalem

According to the Gospels, Jesus and his disciples routinely walked to and from Jerusalem and Bethany almost daily in the last week of Jesus' life. They left Jerusalem late evening for Bethany and returned very early morning from Bethany to Jerusalem, apparently to rest and sleep there. With the unfriendly terrain, it would take about 6-8 hours each way, which made the trip to Bethany useless since there was no time to lie down.

The Greek mastermind realized this blunder after publishing the three Synoptic Gospels and **lied in the Gospel of John** that Bethany was less than three kilometers from Jerusalem.

(John 11: 18) (V2B Ch 2; V2B Ch 17; V2B Ch 18; etc.)

+++

## The Last Supper

On the fateful night after the Last Supper, Jesus and the eleven disciples walked 3400 feet from Jerusalem to Kidron Valley and 3500 feet up the Mount of Olives. They then walked down to Gethsemane, where Jesus was arrested and taken back to Jerusalem. Only after all these events was Jesus tried by the Sanhedrin, a 71-judge court. After that, Peter denied Jesus three times before morning when the rooster crowed.

The last supper ended only around midnight. As per the story of Jesus, it would take at least 15 hours from midnight to the rooster-crowing-morning, but you will know this only if you know the geography, the distances involved between the places, and the mode of transport in those days.

The Greek Mastermind, acting as Luke and writing the Book of Acts, realized this trap in his synoptic Gospels and lied in the Book of Acts that Mount Olives was 1.1 km from Jerusalem (Acts 1:12).

The Greek Mastermind further manipulated the story in the Gospel of John. He claimed that Jesus and his disciples did not climb the Mount of Olives but went straight to an olive grove, deceptively not mentioning the name Gethsemane.
(John 18: 1)
(V2B Ch 2; V2B Ch 17; V2B Ch 18; etc.)
+++

# Jesus' Dilemma: Jews are Greeks, Babylon is Rome, Paul is Peter

## Sanhedrin

# The Sanhedrin

The Jewish high court of justice consisted of 71 men and was led by the high priest. The council could decide almost any fate of its people—except the death penalty, which was decided by the Romans. The court was located within the Chamber of Hewn Stone inside Herod's Temple.



Sanhedrin is a Jewish Supreme Court with 71 judges. They sit only during the day on weekdays, and they do not sit on holidays. As per the Gospels, Jesus was arrested on Friday morning, the second day of the Passover holidays, possibly around 3 AM at Gethsemane, bringing Jesus to Jerusalem by 5 AM. Then Sanhedrin heard the case and decided that Jesus must die, not by crucifixion, as that is prohibited in Jewish Law. The Gospels do not explain why and how the Sanhedrin was sitting and hearing the case before the rooster crowed on the Passover holiday.

(V2B Ch 2; V2B Ch 17; V2B Ch 18; etc.)

+++

# Jesus' Dilemma: Jews are Greeks, Babylon is Rome, Paul is Peter

## Trial of Jesus by the Roman Governor, Pontius Pilate

Apostle John was the only Apostle who witnessed the crucifixion of Jesus. According to all three synoptic Gospels, Jesus was crucified at 12 noon on Good Friday at Golgotha, which was at least one hour away from Jerusalem. Knowing the impossibility of the timing, the Gospel of John claimed that Pontius Pilate made the decision to crucify Jesus only at 12 noon.

Jews never crucified anybody since Jewish Laws prohibit death by torture.
Roman Governor Pontius Pilate did not want to punish Jesus. Romans crucified only those who rebelled against the Roman Empire. Jesus only predicted that Jesus would be killed. The New Testament does not explain why Jews who were baptized "en masse," healed, cured, and fed by Jesus, and who sang "Hosanna" for Jesus would cry on Good Friday to "crucify Jesus," a process they reject.
(V2B Ch 2; V2B Ch 17; V2B Ch 18; etc.)
+++

## Palestine Under the Herods, 4 B.C to A.D. 44

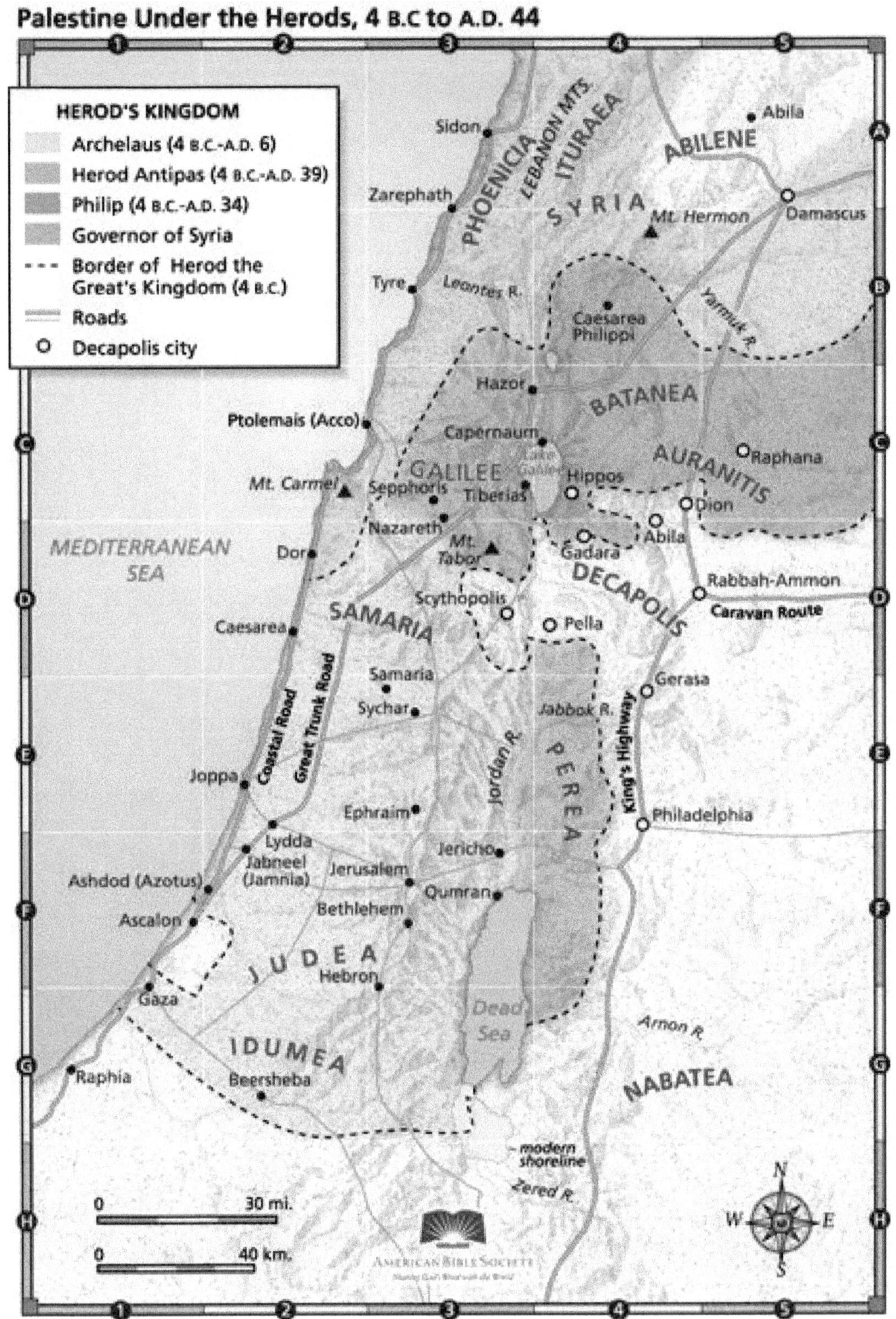

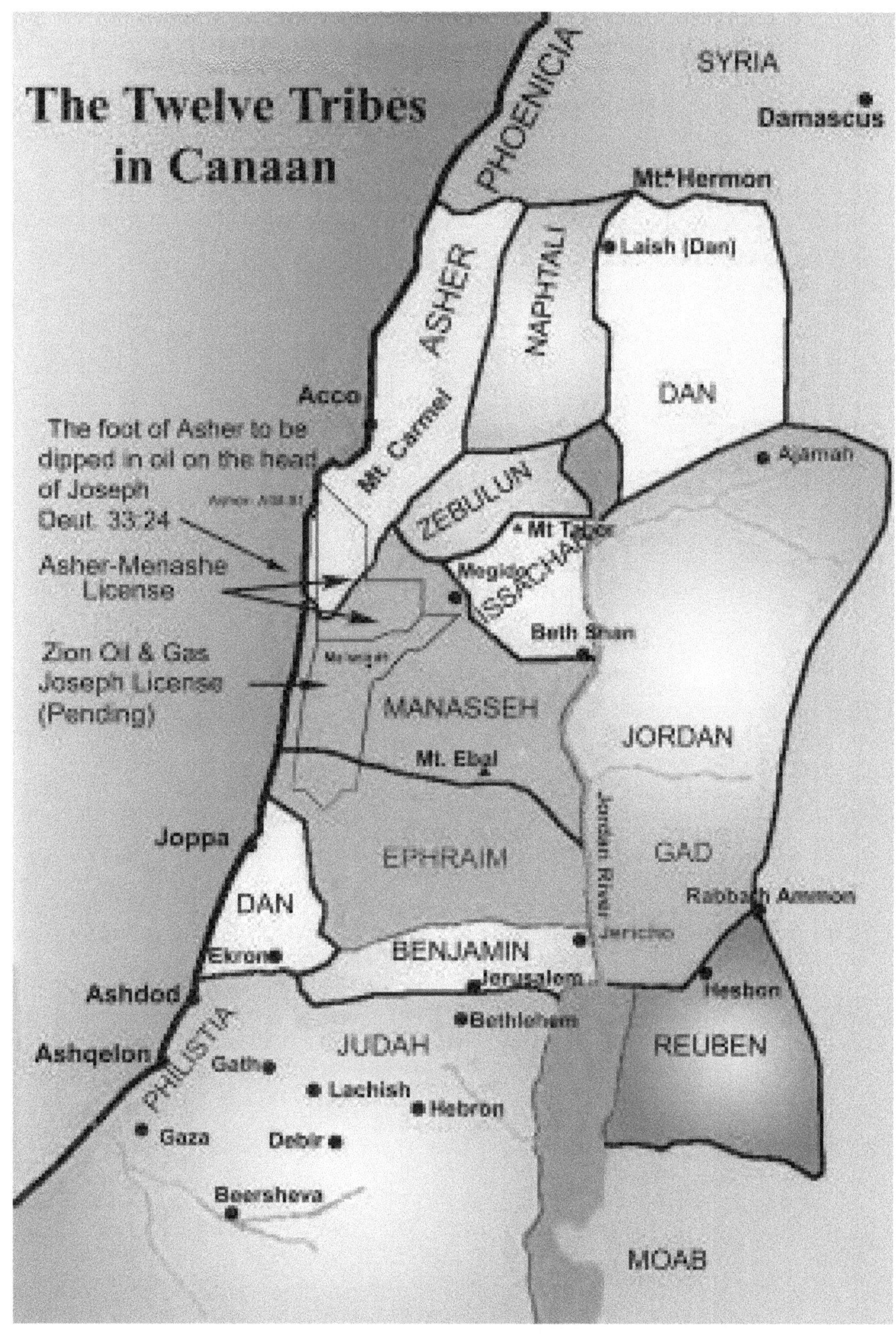
The Twelve Tribes
in Canaan
SYRIA
Damascus
PHOENICIA
Mt. Hermon
Laish (Dan)
ASHER
NAPHTALI
DAN
Acco
The foot of Asher to be
dipped in oil on the head
of Joseph
Deut. 33:24
Asher-Menashe
License
Zion Oil & Gas
Joseph License
(Pending)
Mt. Carmel
ZEBULUN
Mt Tabor
ISSACHAR
Megiddo
Beth Shan
Ajamah
MANASSEH
JORDAN
Mt. Ebal
Joppa
EPHRAIM
GAD
DAN
Ekron
Jordan River
BENJAMIN
Jericho
Rabbah Ammon
Ashdod
Jerusalem
Heshon
Bethlehem
Ashqelon
Gath
JUDAH
REUBEN
Gaza
Lachish
Hebron
Debir
Beersheva
MOAB

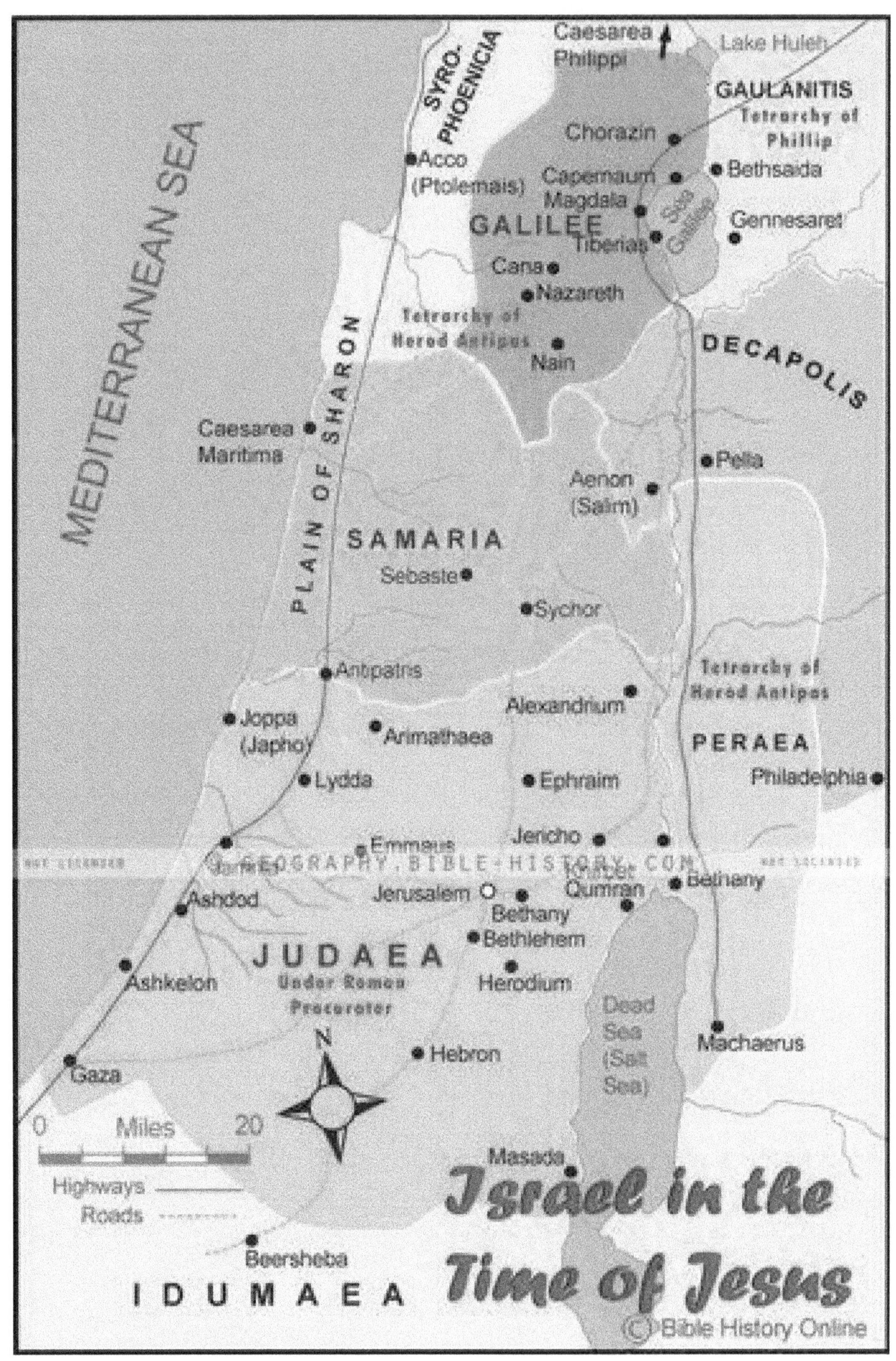

MEDITERRANEAN SEA
SYRO-PHOENICIA
Caesarea Philippi
Lake Huleh
GAULANITIS
Tetrarchy of Phillip
Chorazin
Acco (Ptolemais)
Capernaum
Magdala
Bethsaida
GALILEE
Sea of Galilee
Gennesaret
Tiberias
Cana
Nazareth
Tetrarchy of Herod Antipas
DECAPOLIS
Nain
PLAIN OF SHARON
Caesarea Maritima
Pella
Aenon (Salim)
SAMARIA
Sebaste
Sychor
Antipatris
Alexandrium
Tetrarchy of Herod Antipas
Joppa (Japho)
Arimathaea
PERAEA
Lydda
Ephraim
Philadelphia
Emmaus
Jericho
GEOGRAPHY.BIBLE-HISTORY.COM
Bethany
Ashdod
Jerusalem
Qumran
Bethany
Bethlehem
JUDAEA
Under Roman Procurator
Herodium
Ashkelon
Dead Sea (Salt Sea)
N
Hebron
Machaerus
Gaza
0 Miles 20
Masada
Highways
Roads
Israel in the
Beersheba
Time of Jesus
IDUMAEA
(C) Bible History Online

## Missionary Journeys of Paul

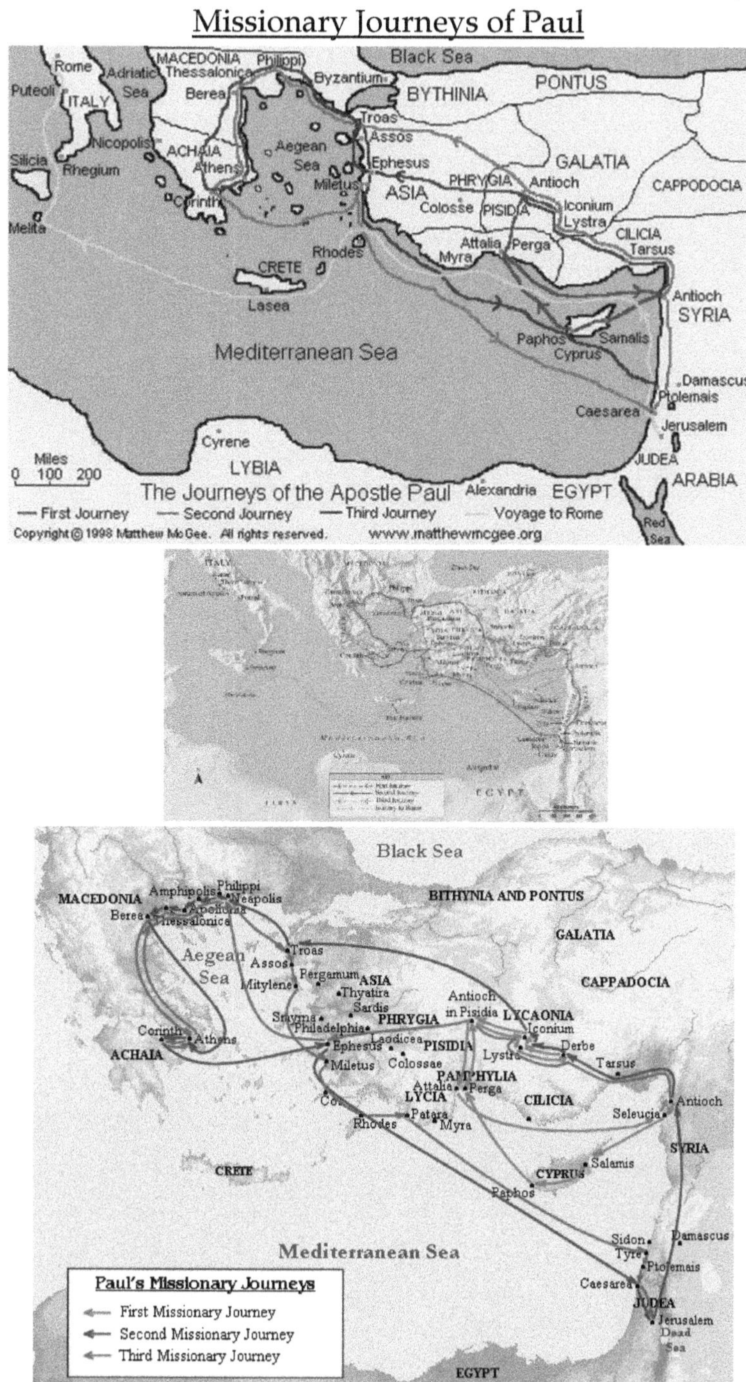





Spain is not even on the map. Apostle Paul, or people in the first century AD in Israel, did not know any land beyond Rome and did not know about Iberia or Hispania, the area today covering Spain and Portugal.  The name "Spain" came about only in 1492.

## Paul's Trip to Rome

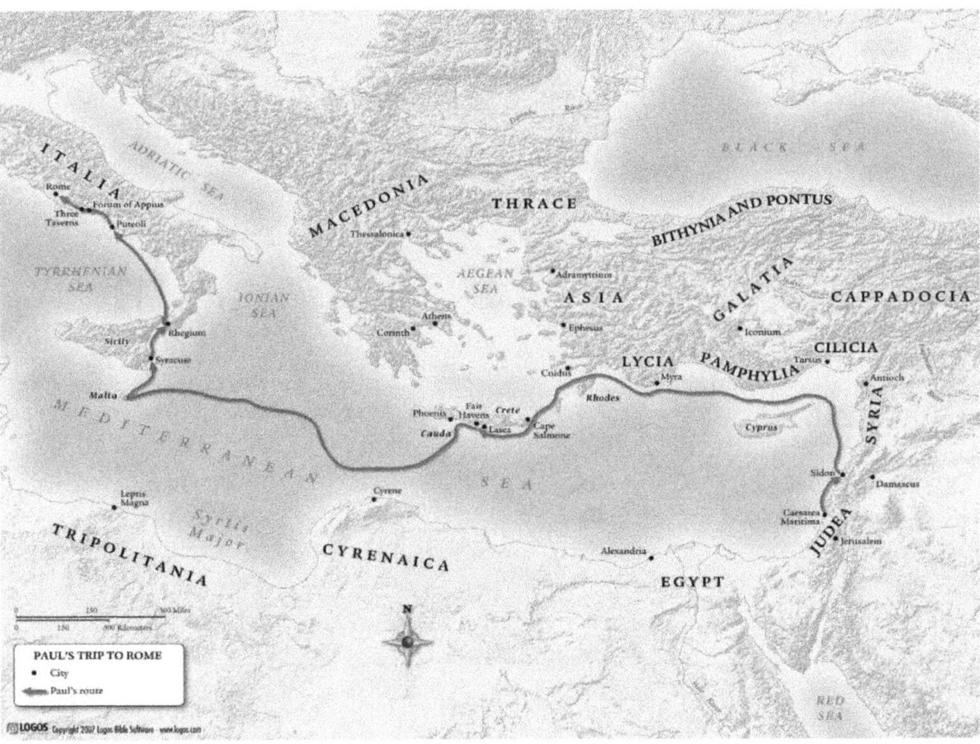


The New Testament claims that Apostle Paul was sent to Rome to be tried by the Caeser on appeal when the three entitles in Judea, Israel, Roman Governor Felix, Roman Governor Festus, and Jewish King Agrippa did not find him guilty, which makes any appeal a non-starter. The trip to Rome was to create a storyline that the Apostle Paul preached in Rome and thereby established a church in Rome.

+++